EVERGREEN

MIRACLES

Larry R. and
Lisa Gleave Laycock

Illustrated by Tannie Gleave Flammer

Dedicated to the Miracle of Memory

With each passing day, we carefully carve scenes in our life's masterpiece. Our minds etch experiences upon ageless souls, and our hearts carve meaning out of those experiences. Some memory carvings we openly display, while others we lock up and hide. If we allow them to, the scenes from our past can emerge to teach us. And it is eternally true that in remembering our past, we discover meaning for our future.

To a child, memory is but a promise—an uncarved piece of wood. Then, over time, we carve an image of life in the form of memories. The wise collect these memories, always sorting them but never discarding them. For, it is in the keeping of our memories that we come to know that love and life are miraculous gifts that will last forever.

ISBN 0-9648178-1-0

MOONWATER PRODUCTIONS

For speaking engagements please call
(801) 763-1824
or fax (801) 763-1856

A portion of the proceeds from the sale of this book
will be shared with those in need.

Chapters

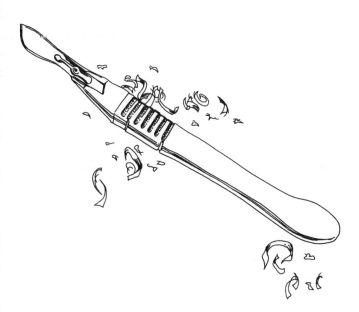

Beginning

Without looking at the carvings on the length of pine tree trunk he held, Dr. Desmond Robert Thomas moved his hands slowly across the rough etchings he had made twenty-six years before. He had begun carving on the pine in a happier, faraway life when he was only seven years old. Robbie, as he was called then, had used a treasured pocketknife that was still among the items placed daily in his trouser pockets. Today, to sharpen the details of the carving, he used a round-edged scalpel. He had intended the carving to be a Christmas gift for his dad in that faraway time, but he had abruptly abandoned it, nearly a year after he'd begun.

The carving was not the only thing Robbie Thomas had abandoned so long ago. With the occurrence of a single tragic incident, he had relinquished all hope and love. Along with the pine carving, Robbie had surrendered his faith and had chosen to rely on one remaining belief—a snow-cold conviction that there were no more miracles in the world, nothing more to believe. Over the years, truth had turned to lies, and faith had faded into forgetfulness.

Yet, he had carefully preserved his unfinished carving all these years. How fitting that he would choose today—Christmas Day—to begin again.

———

"What do you mean you don't *do* Christmas?"

"Just what I said. There was a time when I believed in Christmas and miracles, but that all changed."

"It changed?"

"You have to understand that I have never

really experienced a Christmas with expensive gifts or celebration. I grew up a poor kid, but I never knew it. I believed that my family lived on the wrong side of the tracks because Dad didn't want to live in the city. I thought creamed tuna over toast was a delicacy because we could afford to have it only once in a while. We could eat off just one plate at a time, so we had no need for more than four place settings in our farmhouse. It was the same with clothes. I could wear only one pair of jeans at a time, so that's all I had. Once I asked if we were poor, and Mom said, 'A man's poor only if he wants more than he has.' I believed her until I discovered the depth of our poverty. I felt betrayed. And Mother still thinks we weren't poor."

Dr. Thomas spoke as precisely as he carved. He sat in an oversized black leather chair next to a massive fireplace outlined in white marble. While he talked, he occasionally looked up from his weathered pine stump. Its surface was partially covered with intricate carvings that were hidden by his huge hands. His guest, Liberty Taylor, strained to see the curious evergreen stump and its carvings.

As he carved, Liberty surveyed Dr. Thomas's home. She had immediately noticed there was very little warmth in the expansive gathering room because so little heat escaped the dying fire. The entire wall opposite them was of pane glass windows overlooking the city. Through the haze outside, Liberty could see thousands of muted colored lights twinkling greetings to Christmas morning.

Near the windows, two overstuffed leather chairs faced each other, but only one of the chairs showed signs of use. A bare hardwood floor stretched out across the room to the kitchen, which was obscured by early-morning shadows. Dark gray granite countertops lay on top of and underneath rows of darkly stained cherry cabinets. Orderly lines of unimaginative paintings clung to sanitized, whitewashed walls, and an overabundance of plates and crystal goblets sat in neat stacks behind glass cabinet doors. They appeared unused.

On the far side of the room, a couch, also upholstered in rich black leather, sat vacant in front of a huge stereo with tall, intimidating speakers. Among all these symbols of wealth sat the most curious object of all, Dr. Desmond Robert Thomas. His feet were covered in wood shavings, and he concentrated equally on the conversation and on his carving.

Liberty suddenly wondered what on earth she was doing here. Eleven months had passed since Dr. Thomas had bought, remodeled, and moved into his elegant Avenues house. Liberty correctly surmised that she was the first and only guest the place had known.

The petite nurse had immediately noticed the absence of a Christmas tree, or for that matter, any sign of Christmas in the house. But then, given the doctor's Scrooge-like behavior in the emergency room where they had worked together over the past year, the absence of Christmas failed to surprise Liberty at all, though it did trouble her.

In fact, the only surprising aspect of Dr. Thomas's home was its costly decor. At the hospital he was a miser—obsessed with the possibility of not getting paid for his work. Once Liberty had seen him confront the family of a dying patient to explain that if the man died, the family would still be obligated to pay. He hated the law that often forced him to treat uninsured patients, and he made no attempt to hide his contempt for poverty. The contrasts in his character were, Libby decided, completely irreconcilable, because despite his financial obsession, Dr. Thomas cared deeply for his patients. There were moments when Liberty had even felt close to him.

"What do you think, Ms. Taylor?"

"Oh . . . well, I think that . . . uh . . . maybe you just didn't get around to it," she lied.

"Please, call me Liberty. It suits me better." Actually, all her friends called her Libby, but she didn't think Dr. Thomas considered her a friend.

"I didn't get around to what, Liberty?"

"To decorating for Christmas."

"I told you, I don't *do* Christmas." He put down his carving, walked to the long row of windows and stared silently out of a single pane, focusing on the lights and the snow-covered buildings below. Most of his hours not spent at the hospital were spent alone in front of these windows, observing the slow, methodic movements of the city. The view from the city's east-side avenue seemed eternal, stretching out across the valley floor to the lake and beyond.

"I want to know what you think of a mother who told her son that Santa helped make ends meet. I want to know what you think of a mother who won't tell the truth to her son, not what you think of the absence of a Christmas tree in my home," Dr. Thomas continued.

"I'm sorry. I misunderstood you," Libby replied as she scrambled to formulate a response. "Your mother didn't really lie to you. She just didn't . . ."

". . . tell me the truth. So, it's all right to deceive as long as you don't come right out and lie. Is that what you think, Liberty? Sort of like telling kids there's a Santa Claus?"

Libby felt uncomfortable. She didn't know why Dr. Thomas had invited her to his home. She ought to have refused his invitation last night, but she must have been caught up in the magic of Christmas Eve, because she had actually thought she'd seen a flicker of life in the doctor's dead eyes last night.

Christmas Eve was typically a slow night at the emergency room. Most people stay safely at home with their families, but last night had been anything but slow. A magnificently dressed Santa Claus carrying a sickly beggar woman had visited the hospital, followed by a bunch of homeless people—just the sort of patients Dr. Thomas loathed. But there had been something miraculous about Dr. Thomas's reaction. Of course, the TV cameras Santa had slyly brought with him to film "the doctor who helps homeless patients free of charge on Christmas Eve" hadn't hurt. Santa must have been familiar with Dr. Thomas's prideful ways. But when the cameras had gone, the doctor really had seemed changed. He had seemed more real— more alive. He had seemed almost—happy.

In the leftover glow of the Christmas magic that Santa and his beggar woman had gathered, Libby had worked side by side with Dr. Thomas nearly all night. So when he had invited her to Christmas brunch at his home, she had accepted. And she had decided she would give him the gift she had planned for him—an elegantly carved ornament in the shape of a Christmas tree. Now she wondered why. He was the same miserable person he'd always been. She had been right in telling the beggar woman it would take a miracle to change him.

Liberty was confused. Their relationship had always been strictly work, but now Dr. Thomas had invited her to his home. For what? He had already told her he didn't *do* Christmas.

He wants my opinion about his mother and Santa Claus? He's not changed, and I don't want to stay here any longer. She told herself to relax, but true to the tales of redheads with tempers and true to her feelings of disappointment in the miserly doctor, she couldn't restrain herself. She gathered her belongings as she spit out what she thought of his poor attitude.

"Look here, Dr. Thomas. I don't know what you're trying to do, but you'll never convert me to your way of thinking. I love everything about Christmas and Santa Claus. I love the snow, how it gets slushy and muddy, and freezes my feet through my boots and splashes on my clothes in the street. I love to smell car exhaust mingled with the scent of pine at the crowded Christmas tree lot. And the frenzied shopping—I adore it. Excitement breathes life. My favorite pastime during the month of December is spending money—frivolously. Sometimes I even stoop so low as to drop a few bucks in the Salvation Army donation buckets. And Santa Claus is the best part of it all. He's a jolly old man who spends his life making gifts for others. He's incredible—warm, loving and unselfish—and he's real. But you don't believe, do you? You think you were a poor kid? Guess what, Mr. Doctor, with your shiny red sports car and your fancy furniture, you're still a poor kid. Your mother told you the truth. You just didn't believe her. You don't *do* Christmas? What a crock!" She huffed out of the door and slammed it behind her. Then she reopened it and tossed in the carved Christmas tree ornament. "Merry Christmas, Dr. Thomas." And she was gone.

Dr. Thomas calmly picked up the block of pine and resumed his carving. He resituated himself in the black leather chair by the fireplace and held his scalpel up to the light. His view now included Liberty Taylor, who was trudging ungracefully down the long row of snow-covered steps that led from his front door to the street where her aging brown Toyota waited.

Dr. Thomas looked at the small tree ornament and stretched his long legs out in front of him. He set down his scalpel and wood, clasped his hands in back of his head, leaned back as far as the leather chair allowed, and laughed out loud. He laughed uncontrollably. He laughed until his sides hurt and tears trickled onto his gray tie. His laughter bounced back and forth from marble to hardwood, and none of the walls in his house seemed to know what to do with the unfamiliar sound. He felt blood pumping through his veins, tingling forcefully from his heart to his head and into his fingers and toes. He was finally convinced that Libby's belief was strong enough for both of them. He was beginning a journey back to a life he'd once known, and Santa Claus, of all people, had set him in motion. It was a miracle, and he wanted the feeling to live forever.

Emerging

The tears came without warning as Libby escaped Dr. Thomas and his miserable Christmas brunch. Thinking of brunch reminded her that she hadn't eaten since yesterday at this time, and she was suddenly famished. Safely inside her car, she checked her face in the rearview mirror.

"So there, Dr. Thomas," she said out loud, wiping her tears with her fingers. "I *do* love

Christmas, and thanks to you, my eyes are displaying its colors." Libby's green eyes were usually bright and clear, but the absence of sleep and the presence of tears now clouded and reddened them. Fatigue and hunger always made Libby more emotional, but she rarely let it reduce her to tears. Her trusty Toyota started right up, and she drove away.

She passed rows of houses, many with families outside testing their new Christmas treasures. Several children outfitted in new coats, hats, mittens and boots were pulling sleds. Others were attempting to ride their new bicycles through the slush. A tiny girl, still in a red Christmas nightie, stood knee-deep in front-yard snow, chomping on what looked like a huge icicle.

Everyone seemed so happy. Libby's tears came again. This time, sobs accompanied them. Try as she might, she couldn't control herself.

What is his problem? Libby was embarrassed that she'd acted so irrationally toward Dr. Thomas, but she couldn't understand why he always had to be so negative. She thought she had seen a change last night when she and Dr. Thomas had helped the homeless people that Santa had brought them. Several times she had silently thanked Santa for giving the doctor some needy people. The gift had changed him, or so Libby had thought. When the skinny little homeless girl had offered to share her only Christmas gift—a red glove—with him, Libby thought it had touched his heart. When the child laid her head on his shoulder and he held her and stroked her curly hair, Libby was certain that she had seen a magical transformation in him.

That was why she had accepted his invitation to brunch. Libby had always admired Dr. Thomas. He was a skilled physician, so precise and so intelligent. He knew his practice thoroughly, and his ability to work under pressure was unmatched. She had respected his work from the first time she had seen him perform.

The doctor was also nice looking, all six feet, four inches of him, but to Libby, his hands were his greatest asset. She always noticed men's hands because a person can tell a lot about a man by his hands. Dr. Thomas's hands were unusually large and could have been clumsy, but despite their size, they could deftly suture wounds and do the most delicate of emergency surgeries with masterful precision. They were fairer than the rest of his olive skin on account of the constant handwashing required of a doctor. Libby had also noticed that his right hand was severely scarred, and she often wondered what had happened but never dared ask. She knew that the injury had to have been a terrible one to have left such a mark. Perhaps the wound on his hand had something to do with the scar on his heart.

As Libby drove, she cried and mourned for Dr. Thomas's lifeless heart. She also mourned her own loss of hope that perhaps the doctor could change. Her mistake had been in thinking that last night's Christmas miracle could last. Now she realized she'd been foolish to think that Santa's few homeless people and a skinny little girl could change what seemed to have been a lifetime of anger and bitterness.

Libby's conviction that all humans want to do good, they just don't always know how, could usually sustain her through any situation. She believed that even the most rebellious of hearts holds a desire to be better—the desires just get buried under piles of guilt, shame, and anger. She was convinced that if children were shown how to do good, they would remember it always.

Because of her convictions, Libby donated her time away from the hospital as a volunteer downtown at the School with No Name, a place where homeless children attended school even though they never had the luxury of staying in one place very long.

The children attended the school because they were homeless. But Libby was determined that even though many children left the shelter still homeless, no child would ever leave the shelter still friendless. She knew that to live in a friendless world is a hell no child should ever have to experience. So, she never gave up on any child, no matter how angry or withdrawn the child seemed to be. She shared her heart and her tears with the children, and they shared what they could with her. She knew she could help them. But with Dr. Thomas it was different. She felt helpless.

Libby eased her aging Toyota into the carport of the house that had been her home since she was five years old. She thought about the day her mother had told her she just couldn't raise a child by herself in an unforgiving world any longer. Though life with her mother had been an endless bout with alcoholism, Libby loved her mother and begged her to stay. But one week before Liberty's fifth birthday, her mother left her. And since no one even knew where her father was, Libby had ended up with Gran.

In her memory, Libby knew her mother's face. Even though she'd never seen her mother since that day, she always believed that her mother had wanted to do the right thing; she just didn't know how. Growing up with Gran had convinced Libby that, given the circumstances, her mother really had done the best thing. She stared at the little house that had become her home.

Every window twinkled with bright Christmas lights. Without thinking, Libby ran from her car and into the waiting sanctuary. Inside the door, she dropped her things in the entryway and looked for Gran, who sat in the middle of the large sofa in the living room, surrounded by the Christmas cards she had received this year and in years past. She read them and reread them, savoring every word and every beautiful Christmas scene. Next to her, a tiny Christmas tree displayed festive colors of blue, green, and red. Libby looked sadly at the blank spot left by the absence of her favorite ornament, the one she had given to Dr. Thomas. Brightly wrapped bundles beneath the tree were separated into two stacks. Tradition had always been that Santa, upon arriving with his Christmas bounty, separated the presents so that the task of unwrapping could be more easily accomplished on Christmas morning.

Libby looked lovingly at Gran, who peered down through her glasses and remained engrossed in her reading. Beyond her, two places were decoratively prepared at the large dining room table. Near the table, the hearth and the mantelpiece were decorated with swaths of angel hair, giving the appearance of deep snow. Figurines were arranged on the hearth in a beautiful winter scene of chapel, ice pond, and skaters. Gran had arranged her delicate collection of angels on the mantle, and each of them seemed to smile at Libby, wishing her a Merry Christmas.

Gran's home resonated with warmth. The soft lights from the Christmas tree beckoned Libby, and a glow escaped the yule log burning in the fireplace. Delicious aromas of hot gingerbread and Christmas turkey floated from the tiny kitchen. Libby was home.

Libby loved Gran. Gran was humming, as usual. Her tunes were never recognizable, at least not to Libby, but they were always soothing. Gran had stopped humming for a while after Gramps died, years ago, and Libby remembered yearning for the sweet sound to return. Finally, months later it had. Then life became just the two of them—Gran and Liberty—and they were the best of friends.

Liberty thought of her mother again. She returned often to the good memories of her mother, even though they were few. Now and then Libby still coaxed Gran to tell her about her mother. She especially liked hearing Gran say that she and her mother looked an awful lot alike.

Libby sat down in the blue wingback chair across from the couch, and Gran jumped when she glanced toward her granddaughter.

"Good heavens child, you nearly scared my apron off!" Gran immediately put down her Christmas cards and felt the need for food. Gran always felt the need for food when someone came to her home. "Come into the kitchen with me and tell me about your brunch date with the handsome doctor." Gran set some milk and muffins on the kitchen table. Libby stuffed a moist muffin into her mouth as fast as she could. She took a gulp of cold milk and swallowed hard.

"You obviously didn't eat much." Gran observed out loud.

"Oh Gran, you don't want to know." Tears filled Libby's eyes.

"I don't?" Gran questioned matter-of-factly. "Okay."

Gran went on humming and readying Christmas dinner.

"It was horrible, Gran." Libby sighed between bites and drinks. Gran hid her smile from Libby and continued humming.

"Oh, you don't say?" Gran knew never to try to force Libby into anything, least of all a conversation. She also believed that her lemon poppy-seed muffins could loosen any tongue. When she wanted to extract information from someone, she served homemade lemon poppy-seed muffins with ice cold milk. The person always talked. If she didn't like the guest and wanted to get rid of him or her quickly, she served store-bought cookies with water. And when Gran just needed a sympathetic ear, it was chewy peanut butter brownies and no drink. To Gran, food was serious business. Libby wiped her eyes with the cloth napkin Gran had placed by her plate.

"These muffins are delicious, Gran. And don't think for a minute I don't know what you're up to. Stop pretending you're not interested, and come sit down."

"Yes, of course dear, if you say so." Gran made herself comfortable at the table and searched her granddaughter's green eyes.

"Gran, I just can't figure this guy out. He wants to do good in many ways. He just doesn't know how. He treats his patients lovingly. He's smart. He's . . ."

". . . handsome?" Gran whispered.

"Yes, Gran, but he's a toad. He's mad at his mother because he thinks she lied to him about Santa Claus, for heaven's sake. He's mad at the hospital because we treat homeless people free on Christmas Eve. He's mad at the world because he grew up a poor kid and lived on the wrong side of the tracks. He worships money. His little red sports car means more to him than any person in his life. You should see his house. It's so beautiful it's creepy, but everything in it is dead—just like he is."

"Well, he must not be all dead, or my granddaughter wouldn't be so attracted to him."

"That's just it, Gran. Sometimes I see something in his eyes, like last night at the hospital. He treated one of the homeless children, and she climbed up on his knee. She felt safe with him—I could tell that when she laid her little head on his shoulder. I swear he seemed changed. But today, he was the same miserable man he usually is."

"Perhaps you need to get to know him better."

"Not a chance of that. I blew it today. I let him have it. Then I left."

"If he's the man for you, my dear, he'll not be discouraged by your outburst. I'm sure he's observed your flair for dramatics on other occasions."

"You're right, Gran. He has seen me lose it once or twice." She looked at her grandmother's questioning eyes. "Okay, so he's seen me lose it more than once or twice. But after this morning he must think I'm completely looney. He'll never speak to me again."

"Come now, Liberty, don't cry. We still have our gifts to open. Let's go into the parlor and enjoy our Christmas. He came, you know."

"Who came, Gran?"

"Santa Claus, of course."

"Gran, I'm sorry. I've spoiled Christmas for you."

"Nothing could spoil Christmas for me, dear. The turkey's in the oven, and the pies are fresh baked. We'll have a wonderful rest of the day."

"Thanks, Gran. Do you know how very much I love you?" Libby hugged her grandmother and kissed her cheek.

Gran and Libby slowly unwrapped their gifts to the tunes of Christmas carols, being careful not to tear a single colorful wrapping so Gran could use the paper again next year. While they unwrapped, they visited Christmases past. Then they devoured their memories as they enjoyed Christmas dinner. And finally, they hummed as they cleared the table and washed the china and silverware.

Each time the phone rang, they both held their breath, hoping it was Dr. Thomas. The sixth caller, Uncle Fred and his family, sang all the way through *Jingle Bells* before Libby could overcome her disappointment enough to speak. Then she just mumbled, "Merry Christmas. I'll get Gran." Gran explained that Libby had worked Christmas Eve night and was exhausted.

Dr. Thomas didn't call on Christmas Day. Nor did he call the next day. Libby thought about Dr. Thomas and the Christmas Eve miracle. Oh, how she wished that the feeling could live forever.

Loving

For an instant Dr. Thomas hesitated, looking longingly at Libby's Christmas offering. Then he closed his eyes and thought about Libby. He knew she was a believer, like his mother. Yesterday's Christmas Eve fog had rolled in with the storm, pouring into the valley and clinging to everything in its path. As the sun had set, the fog's misty presence had cast a canopy of uncertainty over the streets and walkways.

Even familiar ground had seemed strange and unrecognizable. Silvery wisps of transparency had tangled themselves around every object, even the light. And although voices and sounds made their way slowly through the labyrinth of clouds, even they had been somehow transformed. Christmas Day now found Dr. Thomas surrounded by a fog of hidden memories that had been patiently awaiting his return. For many years he had been unable to find his past, but now in his mind he followed the dirt path from the detached garage to the back door of his childhood home. The cloudy memories filled his senses.

Robbie Thomas visited his boyhood home just as it had been—worn, yet clean. It was cluttered but somehow orderly. Snow covered the yard and lay in mounds near the back porch. On the frozen path between the house and the ramshackle garage, he found a perfectly shaped rabbit made of snow. The rabbit was wearing an old sweater and scarf. His little sister was always making animals and other objects out of snow and dressing them up as playmates. The only part of her antics that bothered him was that she always used his clothes to dress and warm her snowy friends. Other people made fun of her strange snow art, but he thought it was sort of neat.

The kitchen window glowed warm in the fading light of dusk and beckoned Robbie to the warmth of dinner simmering on the stove. He opened the screen door and then the worn wooden door and hurried inside. His fingers were bright red, numb from the cold, gloveless task of woodcarving that he had been working on in the secret of the family garage. He intended his carving to be a Christmas surprise for his dad.

Robbie saw his dad sitting at the kitchen table reading the newspaper, and he heard his mom chopping vegetables for the salad. Potatoes boiled on the stove, and he smelled meat loaf in the oven. His five-year-old sister, Elizabeth was attempting to spread cold butter on freshly sliced bread. But the butter didn't cooperate, and she slashed holes from crust to crust. Robbie's dad, Desmond Robert Thomas Sr., looked up at his son with questioning eyes.

"What're you workin' on out there, Son? Must be pretty important to keep you busy so long." Robbie just smiled and blew on his fingers. *What am I working on, indeed?* The gift was more a feeling than a carving, and he certainly didn't consider it work.

He had started the carving last year during the celebration of his seventh Christmas. All year, whenever he could find a spare minute, he had sneaked into the old garage to whittle away at the pine. He had completed three of the six scenes he had planned for the project, and he needed to hurry to finish the gift by Christmas Day. He could hardly wait to watch his dad's face react to the evergreen masterpiece. Robbie had a gift for working with his hands. He could create such realistic images out of wood that they actually appeared alive. He decided that the ring of figures and objects he was creating for his dad was his finest work ever.

"Yep, it's pretty important, Dad." Robbie winked at his mom. She knew what he was doing, although he hadn't shown the gift to her yet. His head tingled as he thought about giving his gift on Christmas morning. "You'll see soon enough, Dad." He walked around the table and tussled his dad's few remaining hairs, just as his dad always did with him. Then he sat down at the table.

Robbie and Elizabeth laughed, and Lizzy broke into song, "Jingle bells, jingle bells, jingle all the way . . . " Elizabeth had spent lots of time with Robbie the past year as he had carved. In fact, in February she had given him the idea for his second scene. The two children were discussing all the important aspects of life while Robbie carved—which, to a seven- and five-year-old, consist mostly of super heroes, friends, and Santa Claus.

"Do you think he's real, Robbie?" Lizzy had asked one afternoon during a carving session.

"I know he is."

"How do you know? Laura Robbins says he's not. She says it's Mom and Dad."

"Don't be a goof, Liz. Mom says, 'If you don't believe, you won't receive.' Do you wanna take that chance? I sure don't. Besides, what does it hurt to believe?"

"My friends might make fun of me."

"So. Dad says they're not really friends if they make fun of you for what you believe."

"I guess not. Robbie, I love you."

"I love you, too, Liz."

"I'm glad you believe, Robbie. I don't ever want to get old. Laura Robbins says that when you get old, like twenty or something, then you stop believing in everything."

Robbie stopped carving and looked into Liz's brown eyes. "I'm not ever going to stop believing. I'll believe 'til I'm a hundred years old." Liz climbed onto Robbie's lap and laid her curly head on his shoulder.

"You promise?"

"Yep. Swear it on a stack of Bibles." Robbie put up his right hand and pretended to lay his left hand on a stack of Bibles.

"I, Robbie Thomas, swear that I'll never stop believing, even when I get old."

Then Lizzy took her turn, making the same sacred gesture. "I, Lizzy Thomas, swear that I'll never get too old to believe."

Then they shook hands and grinned at each other. Lizzy was satisfied. As she climbed down off her brother's lap, Mr. Thomas walked in. He had overheard their oaths. He smiled, "Those are the most important promises I've ever heard."

Robbie struggled to conceal his evergreen gift.

His discussion with Lizzy and the promises they made to one another gave Robbie the idea for the second scene in his ring of carvings. He drew his ideas on paper first and then transferred them to the evergreen trunk. The scene consisted of his little sister Lizzy with her left hand on the Bible and her right hand raised. Carved into the cover of the Bible, underneath *Holy Bible*, were the words, "I Believe."

Desmond Thomas opened his eyes and closed his memory. His visit to the past was painful. His eyes burned, but oddly enough, as the tears came the hurt lessened. He spoke as if his sister could hear him. "Oh little Lizzy, you kept your promise. I miss you. Do you know how much I love you?"

He didn't want to remember any more. The little homeless girl who had talked with such excitement about Santa Claus last night at the hospital had reminded him so much of his little sister that when he had asked her name, he had fully expected her to say, "Lizzy." But she hadn't. Her name was Anna, and she had magically stolen his heart.

"Where is Anna?" He wondered. "The poor kid; she's so alone. At least I've got memories to visit."

Dr. Thomas traced another scene with his fingers, the first scene he'd carved. It was of a simple wooden table and a tiny Christmas tree. It, like the other carved scenes, was linked to the rest by intricate evergreen wreaths. The uneven engravings softened, then blurred, and finally transformed into the reality of his own experience, taking him back again to a happy, believing boy carving in his family's garage.

The forest of evergreen trees behind his childhood home had become a gathering place for those in search of beautiful Christmas trees. The income from the sale of trees each year helped to finance the continuing repairs needed for the Thomases' hay swather and ancient tractor. It also bought a modest Christmas for the family. For a moment, he paused in his memory while he watched his dad meandering through the rows, inspecting his evergreens.

Robbie bounded down the trail to join his dad in selecting the trees that would be sacrificed for the celebration of Christmas. He stopped abruptly to smile at his dad's sign. He was pleased that the sign never said "XMAS TREES" like the lot in town. Instead, the Thomas tree lot always bore a hand-painted sign that read "Christmas Evergreens for Sale."

Only the straightest and best-formed trees would be used to celebrate the birth of God's son. Robbie reached his dad, who instantly took his son's small hand as they walked. "There's a lot more to a Christmas evergreen than just getting something to hang ornaments on. There's a bit of God in these trees."

The tall man took a freshly cut evergreen

and dusted the snow from its branches. "Look at it—this evergreen has spent its whole life reaching for the sun, trying to grow true and strong. Now we'll take it for the Special Season, and it'll keep its color 'til it dies. That's what I want for you, Son." Robbie loved to walk through the trees with his dad and feel the cool mist of snow fall from the evergreen limbs onto his face.

Later that afternoon, the plump mayor and a lean city councilor stopped at the Thomas farm and selected the finest tree on the property to stand in the city hall. The evergreen stood more than thirty feet tall and stretched out in perfect symmetry from top to bottom. Every inch of the magnificent tree was filled with rich, thick foliage.

Robbie's father and the city councilor stood the tree up while the mayor waved his stubby arms up and down with excitement. He proclaimed it "a perfect specimen." But Robbie didn't pay any attention to the mayor's speech. Instead, he concentrated on the jowls jiggling and undulating beneath the mayor's chin. He was sure the mayor's chins would strangle him.

The mayor exclaimed, "That's the one for City Hall this year. We'll send a truck to pick it up within the hour." They laid the tree down.

As the mayor paid Mr. Thomas, the emaciated councilor paced back and forth beside the tree, biting his fingernails and mumbling, "Five, ten, fifteen, twenty, twenty-five, and thirty. Wait just a minute," he stammered. "This tree is too tall by three feet. You'll have to shorten it."

Mr. Thomas handed his son the saw and said, "Little man, do me the favor of taking three feet off that tree." Robbie was proud that his dad would trust him to take care of such an important task. He approached the tree and sawed three feet from the beautifully formed top of the evergreen. Mr. Thomas discovered what was happening only when it was too late, and the mayor and the councilor gasped in unison.

"Robbie, not that end—not the top!" His dad tried to stop him.

It was too late. The small boy turned, holding the saw in one hand and the top of the tree in the other. He smiled until he saw the scowling faces lurching toward him.

The councilor shook his bony fist. "It's destroyed. Look what you've done!"

The mayor turned his massive body toward Mr. Thomas. "This is certainly not the tree we agreed to buy, Thomas. Look at it! It's ruined!"

Mr. Thomas looked at his son, the tree, and the men shaking their fists in Robbie's direction. There was a long pause, and then Mr. Thomas did something the young boy should never have forgotten. He knelt down next to his son. "Thank you for doing as I asked." He stood and turned to the menacing faces. "I apologize. This was my mistake, not my son's." He returned the money. "We'll give the tree to the city, no charge. Don't worry, Mayor, we'll trim the top so it will be acceptable." The mayor held his hand to his chins and then gruffly accepted the offer.

Robbie cried only after the mayor and his councilor were gone.

"I'm sorry, Dad—I didn't know . . . ."

"It's all right, Son. I didn't tell you which end to cut. It's my fault. Besides, you never know what'll come from something like this. All I know is we got one little Christmas tree that needs a place to stay for the holidays." He motioned toward the little tree top and then put his arm around the boy's slumped shoulders. "Don't worry, Son. Things happen for a reason."

The evergreen Christmas tree top waited by the garage, accumulating layers of snow on its delicate branches. As the celebration of Christmas grew nearer, almost every tree was sold from the Thomas lot. Robbie was relieved when the snow almost covered the little tree. He didn't like thinking about the experience with the mayor and the councilor, and he hoped to forget the whole thing.

Mr. Thomas had set part of the stump of the massive evergreen he'd given to the city next to the tree top, and soon the tree and the stump were completely buried under the snow.

Robbie could hardly wait for the yearly tradition of sharing Christmas. His family worked throughout most of the year preparing the items they would share and then, a few days before Christmas, the Thomases filled a bushel basket to the brim and decided which needy family they would visit. A few days before Christmas Mr. and Mrs. Thomas told the children what the family would do to share Christmas with those in need. Mrs. Thomas and Lizzy busily wrapped Kerr bottles. They used brown paper, and ribbons made from twine rope to conceal bottles filled with their autumn's harvest. They placed each carefully wrapped package in a bushel basket until it overflowed with expertly bottled pickles, corn, beans, beets, and venison. Next, Mrs. Thomas folded the exquisite quilt on which she and Lizzy had worked all year. Lizzy tied a bow of twine around it and helped her mother place it on top of the bushel basket.

After Mr. Thomas placed the basket in the

back of the pickup truck, Robbie grimaced as he watched his dad shake the snow from the branches of the little tree top. He also noticed the stump of evergreen.

"Dad, could I have that stump you cut off the city tree?"

"Sure, Son. What do you want it for?"

"Just for fun, Dad. Thanks."

Mr. Thomas fashioned a small tree stand out of a thin strip of plywood. He tapped a nail into the plywood, and with two swinging motions, sank the nail deep into the remaining trunk of the tiny tree. Robbie noticed that his mom had gathered together a single string of lights and some Christmas ornaments that had always hung on the family's Christmas tree. Robbie ran to the garage to stow away his evergreen treasure. He had a plan for the wood, but it would have to wait until he got back. Then they all climbed into the cab of the truck.

The sun was setting as they approached the timbers, a wooded area along a creek leading to the nearby lake. Nestled among the timbers was the Stephenson farm. Deep, unmolested drifts of white covered the road leading to the farmhouse where the old couple lived. In the distance, Robbie could see a wisp of smoke escaping the chimney.

"Who we gonna give all this stuff to, Dad?" Lizzy questioned. She didn't know who the Stephensons were. But Robbie did. Each day he passed their house as he rode his bicycle to deliver newspapers. Some days Robbie noticed old Mrs. Stephenson walking home from the grocery store carrying heavy bags of groceries all by herself. Apparently, the Stephensons didn't have a car. He also noticed that old Mr. Stephenson never came out of the house. His mom said that Mr. Stephenson had a stroke, whatever that was. In any event, he had spied the old man standing next to the window with one of his shoulders slumping and part of his mouth angling downward in a frown. To Robbie, there was no one more frightening than Mr. Stephenson. No one had heard him speak since he'd had his stroke, and Mrs. Stephenson was too busy taking care of her husband to say hello or to talk with anyone.

The Thomas pickup truck pushed its way through the snow to the gate in front of the farmhouse. Mr. Thomas gathered up the bushel basket filled with Christmas treasures. He then told Robbie to bring the tree. Standing on the porch of the Stephenson home, the Thomas family joined hands and sang, "Silent night, holy night. All is calm, all is bright."

The door opened, and light flooded out into the evening air, shining on the entire Thomas family. Mrs. Stephenson stood in the doorway clasping her hands in front of her and smiling. Her eyes glistened. Mr. Thomas hoisted the basket and the precious quilt closer to the doorway, and the old woman motioned them in. Mr. Thomas nodded for Robbie to come forward with the tree, but Robbie was reluctant. He didn't even want to see old Mr. Stephenson, with his drooping eye and frowning face. But he obeyed.

The old home was conspicuously lacking any sign of Christmas. There was no tree. There were no decorations. There were neither smells of rich foods baking in the oven nor aromas of delicacies simmering on the stovetop. No scent of freshly cut pine met their nostrils, and no Christmas music filled their ears. Nothing but a ramshackle wooden table, a backless chair, and a mismatched chair greeted the family. Mrs. Thomas carefully placed the string of lights on the tree. Next, Lizzy helped place as many of the ornaments on the tree as she could reach. Robbie completed the task, hanging his favorite hand-carved, Christmas tree ornament on the highest branch. Then the family sang the final verse of "Silent Night" and prepared to leave. Mrs. Stephenson thanked them, patted Mr. and Mrs. Thomas on the arm and wished them a merry Christmas. Robbie had been pushed farther into the room when he'd put the final ornaments on the little Christmas evergreen, and he was trying to make his way to the door.

Mr. Stephenson cleared his throat several times. He stared intently at the Christmas tree and the lights that dangled from its tiny branches. He looked at Mrs. Stephenson and back at the tree. Then he whispered, "Look, Mama. They brought us Christmas."

Old Mr. Stephenson talked! Robbie looked first at his mom. She was hugging Mrs. Stephenson. Then he saw tears squeezing out of his dad's eyes. He looked at Lizzy. She just stood there with her mouth wide open. Then she moved closer to Robbie and slipped her hand inside his, and he smiled at her. Robbie knew it was a miracle, and he wanted the feeling to last forever.

Each day after that as he passed the Stephenson farmhouse on his way to deliver papers, Robbie noticed that the tree lights shined brightly from the window. In fact, the tree lights remained on every day until the day old Mr. Stephenson died, three weeks later. Sharing Christmas with the Stephensons had touched Robbie's heart, and he had felt what it is to know the spirit of Christmas. It had truly been a bright and holy night.

Dr. Thomas opened his eyes and returned to his expensive Avenues home. This memory had been carved deeply in Dr. Thomas's mind. His senses had recorded it and waited for him to return so it could reveal itself and again touch his heart. He remembered that evergreen as he remembered no other Christmas tree in his life. He also remembered the love that had surged in his soul twenty-six years before. He remembered the little tree lights reflecting in the tear on old Mr. Stephenson's cheek, and he recalled what it meant to share Christmas.

Dr. Thomas no longer feared his memories—in fact, he was finally ready to make his way through the mist and fully unlock them. He knew that good or bad, pleasant or not, they were a part of him, and he needed them. Dr. Thomas stared at the evergreen tree trunk again. Years ago he had carved the image of the Stephensons' table and the evergreen tree top as part of his dad's Christmas gift. The images in his mind matched the carvings on the evergreen stump. Still, one fettered memory remained.

Dr. Thomas had locked up his life's memo-

ries, intending that they be left unvisited forever. But now, as he reluctantly opened a men-
tal window to his long-incarcerated past, he
saw the irregular and roughhewn images of his
life in the shape of a little boy's carvings on an
evergreen tree trunk. Somehow he knew that
the carvings on the evergreen held the key to
his future and could unlock a miracle. Reluctantly, Dr. Thomas closed his eyes and again
returned to his past.

Robbie's eighth Christmas was different
from his seventh. He'd been carving for a year
on the evergreen, but he was only partly finished, and Christmas was only two short
weeks away. He opened the door of the old
Ford pickup truck and hurried Lizzy inside. He
had won the race this time and claimed the
right to sit by the window. Lizzy stuck her
tongue out at her brother and scooted closer to
her dad, tucking her feet behind his. Mr.
Thomas had left the truck running, so it was
warm inside except for the upholstery and
metal dashboard. Robbie turned to the window and gripped the door handle as they
headed into the fog to deliver the last two

Christmas trees. He breathed on the window and began tracing the form of an evergreen tree on the misty surface.

The snowstorm howled through Miner's Pass, and thick fog filled the air. "Whiteout" is what his dad called it when it got like this. And as far as Robbie was concerned, it might as well have been midnight on a moonless night. He watched frantically for the black flags that the Department of Transportation placed along the roads each winter. Every once in a while he glimpsed a flag. His dad concentrated, groping with his eyes to see the next and the next. The snow surrounded them, and the old pickup truck crawled, yet it seemed that they were going faster and faster as they drove into the storm. Robbie wondered whether his dad knew how scared Lizzy seemed to be, but Mr. Thomas didn't seem bothered by the storm. Robbie could see a million streaking starflakes shooting past him out of the nothingness. He imagined that he was traveling through space.

Incredibly, the storm intensified. Heavy snowflakes smothered the lights on the truck, and Mr. Thomas tightened his grip on the cracked steering wheel as they headed up the steep incline on Miner's Mountain. Robbie momentarily forgot his own fear when he felt Lizzy's little fingers dig into his knees. He slid closer to her and put his arm around her.

"We'll be okay, Lizzy. Don't worry, Dad and I will protect you." He looked at his dad for assurance.

"Your brother's right, Lizzy Lou. We'll always take care of you."

Robbie instantly felt better. Lizzy liked the pet name her dad always used for her. She felt safe, and Robbie felt strong.

The fog was thick, and none of them saw the headlights of the eighteen-wheel tractor-trailer until it was too late. Robbie felt paralysis grip him as the semi ripped into the back of the pickup, tearing away the pickup bed and throwing open the driver's door. Lizzy was thrust forward and then backward, striking the windshield and then the seat back. As the pickup rolled, the ceiling came crushing down.

Robbie too was thrown about in the cab, striking his knees on the dash and his head on the ceiling. A piece of metal cut a deep gash along his right hand. When he finally came to, the first thing he saw was blood. It was everywhere. At first he thought it was his own, but he soon realized it was Lizzy's. As he stared at her lifeless body, a cry escaped him. "Lizzy, Lizzy, say something!" His small, torn, and bruised eight-year-old body ached with the recognition that Lizzy was gone, but he refused to believe it. He sobbed and held her tightly.

Finally, after what seemed like hours, two men reached into the wreckage and rescued Robbie, who was still clinging to his sister. Mr. Thomas was found alive by the side of the road. He was having difficulty breathing, and the right side of his chest rose and fell out of synchrony with the left. The men placed Mr. Thomas in the back of a Rambler station wagon. Then they loaded the children into the same car and crept to the nearest hospital.

Coalville Hospital was a twenty-bed, two-doctor facility. There was no emergency department, and at the entrance one of the men rang the shrill doorbell. The nurse answered. She frantically called Dr. Rose's home. Dr. Rose raced out of bed to his car. Coalville Hospital was not equipped to handle true emergencies.

Robbie watched as they took his dad and placed him on one of the two available beds. Then they put Lizzy's body at her father's side. They covered her pretty face with a white sheet, and Mr. Thomas reached for Lizzy with one hand. He stretched his other hand toward his son. He squinted his eyes and looked back and forth at each of them.

Dad, please don't die. Dad, please, be okay. Where

is the doctor? Robbie felt helpless. Everything was moving in slow motion. He watched his dad's breathing become more and more labored. He watched his dad's eyes gradually close. *Where is the doctor? Why is everything taking so long?*

The fog that had caused the accident penetrated Robbie's being. He was unable to escape it. *Why did this happen? What should I do?* He imagined his dad's voice. "Things happen for a reason, Son." The doctor wasn't there and the nurse was no help, except to bandage Robbie's hand. The nurse attempted to notify Mrs. Thomas, but the call would not go through. Wanting to avoid his father's pain, Robbie stumbled out of the hospital room, down the gray sterilized corridor until he came to the door at the end of the hallway. This was nothing like the other doors he'd seen in the hospital. It looked like a hand-carved wooden door. A rose carved from dark wood made up each corner, and the four roses were joined by an exquisite frame of carved rose petals and leaves. The window itself, in the center of the unusual wooden door, was the crystal image of a single rosebud. Soft pink light beckoned through it.

Robbie felt cold, but his tears magnified the light and created the only semblance of warmth he experienced since he'd entered the hospital. He reached out to touch it. His wounded hand made its way along the door's beautiful frame and then onto the glass. The glass felt as warm as it looked, and he rested his cheek on a petal of glass. As he pulled himself toward the door, it opened slowly.

Inside was a small chapel. Three rows of cushioned cherrywood benches were illuminated by a huge chandelier hanging directly above a small pulpit. On the front wall, three cathedral-shaped, stained glass windows reached the ceiling, and a street light shining through the glass revealed an image of Jesus blessing some children.

Robbie wiped his tears to more clearly see the magnificent windows. For a moment, the fog cleared, and he ignored his pain. No one else was in the chapel, and Robbie felt a bit stronger, as he looked into the smiling eyes of the glass Jesus, a carver of wood like himself. He stared at the glass children. One boy in a white robe looked about his own age. The boy had his hand on Jesus's shoulder, and they looked so . . . peaceful.

As Robbie walked to the glass, tears stung his eyes. Slowly, he removed his gloves from his coat pocket and whispered, "I know you can hear me, and I know you can make my dad better." He wiped his eyes with his green wool gloves, and then set them at the foot of the window. "Please help me. I'm so scared. If you'll help my little sister and my dad, you can have my gloves. They're the best I've got." He talked to the window until he was completely exhausted. Finally, the tired boy curled up in a little ball on the front bench of the chapel. Just as sleep soothed his soul, he thought he heard the door of roses behind him, but he was too tired to look. He fell asleep.

When Robbie awoke several hours later, the windows were dark and one of his gloves was gone. He felt cold again. He took his remaining glove as he left the glass Jesus and the children. He walked slowly from the chapel. He had lost too much that night.

Dr. Thomas opened his eyes. He found himself on his knees, sobbing, the pain in his right hand piercing upward toward his heart. He was surrounded by his liberated memories. "All these years, I thought you had left me, but you didn't. I left you. That night I was alone—lost in a fog that wouldn't lift. Forgive me. I am finally finding my way back. Please forgive me."

Among his memories, Dr. Thomas found his faith. Even though he knew only too well that love sometimes hurts, he consciously chose love over the numbness he'd experienced during the past twenty-six years of his life.

"To love is to live, and I will live again," Dr. Thomas vowed. It was a miracle, and he understood that feelings once carved, do live forever.

Illuminating

Desmond was aware that the only thing more difficult than changing himself for the better would be convincing others that he actually had changed. The morning sun peeked into the bathroom window, and he felt so different, but as he brushed his teeth and studied himself in the bathroom mirror, his reflection was the same. He brushed, spit, and rinsed. Then he did something previously unheard of. He smiled. "See, I do look different, and I'll prove it. Today, I'm a new man." He held his hand out to his reflection. "Glad to meet you, Dr. Thomas. I once knew a miserable fool named Dr. Thomas, but I can see you are not that man. By the way, that smile looks good on you." He winked at himself and left the bathroom.

For a man who had slept so little in the past forty-eight hours, he was surprisingly exhilarated. After Liberty had left so abruptly yesterday morning, he'd become engrossed in his carving and his memories. The faster he had carved, the clearer his plan had become. He had thought and carved through the rest of Christmas Day and into the night. When he had awakened, on his knees, he had watched the sun rise and chase the last offspring of mist and fog away. Brilliant light melted away the shimmering remains of the threatening obscurity. Diamonds and crystals enveloped everything—tree branches, shrubs, window panes, and rocks. The rising light glistened through the crystal and bent into rainbows of color cascading across the snow.

Like the fog that lifted, Dr. Thomas's mind cleared for the first time in many years. In the mist of his disbelief and fear, he had been lost, isolated, and alone. His ability to unlock his past had been clouded by a million strands of haze. But his memories, like the sun, now warmed the furthest recesses of his psyche and melted away the icy sheath of purposeful forgetfulness. He was ready to live again.

Desmond had always despised his days away from work. They were painful, lonely days. But today he was thrilled to have a whole day to work his plan. First, he had to find little Anna. He snatched his coat and scarf from the closet and ran to the garage.

"So, Libby Taylor has seen you, old boy," he said to his red sports car. "That's a good sign—means she's been watching us." He jumped inside, and the engine purred softly. Desmond smiled and waved at the children and their new toys as he drove along the same street Libby had passed yesterday. He talked to himself. "I'm going to find Santa Claus. He'll know where Anna is. Yeah, right. Where do I find Santa Claus on the day after Christmas? And why did he bring those homeless people to me?" Desmond laughed. "I need a private investigator . . . Hey, wait a minute. That's not such a bad idea. I'll hire a P.I. to find Mr. C."

Desmond spotted a telephone booth. He swerved behind a snowplow and parked. Thumbing through the yellow pages, he spoke again to himself. "I must be looney." He found a list of names, numbers, and addresses, and he closed his eyes to point one out. "So much for the scientific method. Collin Mathers, P.I.," he read. "Sounds good to me." He punched the numbers and waited. Four rings and still no answer. About to hang up, he heard a woman's monotone voice.

"Lost and Found Detective Agency. You lose 'em, we look for 'em. Who can we find for you today?"

Desmond paused, thinking how unprofessional the place sounded and that he should hang up. Then he thought about what he was going to ask them to do, and he decided that they might just be the ones for the job.

"I . . . well . . . Can you . . . I mean, will you find Santa Claus for me?" He held his breath and waited for her response.

"Okay, bucko." She chewed her gum and deliberately popped it into the phone. "You're the third crackpot who's called here today lookin' for Jolly Old St. Nick. What's the matter, big guy? Santa didn't leave you anything, either? Did you get a lump of coal in your sock, or did you just wanna say thanks?"

"No, you don't understand. I've gotta find the Santa Claus that visited me on Christmas Eve."

"As opposed to the Santa Claus that visited you on Easter? Get a grip, Mister—what did you say your name is?"

Desmond decided to try another approach. He spoke slowly. "My name is Doctor Desmond Robert Thomas. I have a job for a private investigator, and money is no object."

It was the woman's turn to get excited. She almost swallowed her wad of gum, so she spit it into her hand. "I'm very sorry, Mister Money—I mean Mister, Doctor Thomas. I'll put you right through to Mr. Mathers."

Desmond heard the woman put her hand over the phone and shriek, "Collin, Collin! Pick up the phone. We got us a hot one."

Collin Mathers, P.I., was smooth. "Hello. This is Mr. Mathers. How can I be of service?"

Desmond smiled. "Hello, sir. I need your help to find someone."

"You're in luck. You've called the best. I can find anyone, anywhere. Tell me about the lost soul."

At the thought of finding Anna, Desmond grew anxious again.

"No, *he's* not the lost soul. *I'm* the lost soul. I mean, I was the lost soul, but I'm not any-more . . . that is, lost. Santa Claus helped me find myself."

Collin Mathers glanced at his receptionist, who was also his secretary, runner, book-keeper, and wife. He rolled his eyes and shook his head. His wife stuck her gum back in her mouth, grabbed her purse, pulled out a dollar bill and rubbed it between her thumb and forefinger. He nodded his understanding and listened more intently to Desmond's babbling.

"I have to find Santa Claus. He's not just any Santa. He's the real thing. He wears an incredible red suit. His beard and hair are real, not that store-bought or rented stuff. He carries a carved staff that looks exactly like him. He wears real antique spectacles, carries a pipe but doesn't smoke it, and has a red list and a red satin bag. The buttons on his jacket are gold, shaped like holly leaves and stars and Baby Jesus. Oh, and he wears a pair of neat-looking red gloves, and speaks with a Scandinavian accent."

"I'm telling you, he's real. He knew what I wanted for Christmas, and he brought her to me. I didn't even know I wanted her, but Santa did. He knew everything—my name, my selfishness, my ego—everything. He knew I needed her. And she needs me, too."

"Her?"

"Yes, a little homeless child named Anna. Santa Claus brought her to me, but she got away."

"Was she dressed in green, wearing pointy shoes with bells? Did she have big pointed ears?"

"Of course not. She was dressed in rags, wearing worn shoes with no buckles. And she had the cutest little ears I've ever seen. She even offered to share one of her new red gloves with me."

"Let me get this straight, Dr. Thomas. You're looking for the *real* Santa Claus who knows everything. Who brings people small children, wearing rags and brand-new red gloves?"

"No, no. He doesn't bring children to everyone. He brings whatever you need. I needed Anna, so he brought her to me."

"But she got away?"

"Yes, she left before I realized that she was my gift. But now I know, so I have to find her."

"And if you find your real Santa, he can tell you where she is, right?"

"Exactly! Thanks, Mr. Mathers, I knew you'd understand."

"Just so you know, this could get very expensive. Finding the real Santa will not be easy, especially after Christmas." Mr. Mathers waited for a reply, expecting Dr. Thomas to hang up the way most desperate people did whenever he mentioned costs.

"I understand. I'm prepared to pay the cost, whatever it takes."

"You are? Well, I need the money up front.

A thousand bucks, cash only, right now, and I'll find your Santa in twenty-four hours. Guaranteed."

"I'll be right there."

Desmond hung up, scrawled the address on an old prescription pad he found in his pocket, and raced to the bank, and then to Collin Mathers's office. The office was just what he'd expected—a real dump in the wrong section of town. But he didn't care. All he could think of was finding Anna.

Desmond held up ten one-hundred-dollar bills in one hand, and hurried past the woman he'd talked to on the phone. In the other hand, he clutched the tree ornament Libby had given him. The receptionist called after him, "Mister Mathers will see you now. Go right in Doctor Thomas." She really meant, "Go right past me," because the office consisted of only one room.

"I'll have the name and address of Santa Claus within twenty-four hours, or give your money back. Just answer three questions for me. Number one, where did you last see Santa?"

"At Valley Hospital on Christmas Eve. He brought in a sick bag lady and a bunch of homeless people to the ER. I treated them all, but Mr. C. was gone when I finished."

Mathers took notes as Desmond explained.

Then Mathers asked his second question. "Did anyone else see this Santa Claus?" He stopped writing and looked straight into Desmond's eyes.

"Yes, everyone on duty at the hospital saw him. One nurse, Liberty Taylor, saw him very well." Desmond gave Mathers Liberty's phone number. Mathers heaved a sigh of relief to think that at least Santa might not be a figment of Desmond's imagination.

"Okay, and number three. Was Santa Claus driving a sleigh pulled by eight tiny reindeer?"

Desmond finally realized that Mathers was questioning his credibility. But then, why not? After all, he was hiring a P.I. to find the real Santa.

"Of course not."

Mathers seemed relieved, and Desmond continued confidently. "He drove a new, red Chevy Blazer with green holly leaves and pin-striping. I saw it when he drove up to the ER doors to unload the bag lady."

Mathers was encouraged that there were no reindeer but was concerned about the Blazer description. Nobody puts green holly leaves and pinstripes on a brand-new Blazer. "You didn't happen to notice the plates, did you."

"The license plates? No, I'm afraid not."

"Okay. I'll get to work on this right now. I'll put it before my other files." He looked around for his other files but found none. "Oh, I suppose my wife—I mean my secretary—put my files away."

Desmond smiled, shook hands with Mathers, and started out the door. "Twenty-four hours, right? You've got my phone number. Call me if anything happens. And thanks, Mathers. I really appreciate this."

Mrs. Mathers was already on the phone. "Hello. Ms. Taylor please." She paused and winked at her husband who had collected his coat and hat and was headed out the door.

"The dry cleaners?" Mrs. Mathers asked her husband.

"Yep, be right back." There were three dry cleaners in the area of Valley Hospital. Collin would check them all to see if a Santa suit matching Desmond's description had come in.

Rita quickly spit out her gum. "Hello, Ms. Taylor? Are you one of the nurses who worked in the ER at Valley Hospital on Christmas Eve?"

"Yes I am. Who is this, please?"

"My name is Rita Mathers," she answered truthfully. "I'm looking for the Santa Claus who visited the hospital." Then she lied. "We're doing a feature story on him for the *Val-*

ley City Review. Wasn't his suit magnificent? And those antique spectacles were wonderful. Personally, I liked his real hair and beard. But his red Chevy Blazer, with the holly leaves and pinstriping, really topped it off. Do you remember, Ms. Taylor?"

Rita expected Nurse Taylor to say she didn't know what she was talking about, but Liberty laughed. "Oh, that's a wonderful idea. A story on Valley Hospital's Santa. I'll help you in any way I can."

"You will?" Rita sounded astonished. "Yes, of course you will. Did you happen to notice the license plates on his Chevy?"

"You aren't going to reveal who he is, are you?"

"Oh no—we'd never do that. We just have to confirm that he's not some kind of a nut or weirdo."

"Yes, I noticed the license plate. It was perfect, just like he was. I'll never forget. It was I-B-L-E-V."

"I-B-L-E-V?"

"Uh-huh. Cute, isn't it?"

"I don't get it."

"You know, *I believe*."

"Oh, how clever. I should have known. I think I like this Santa who performs miracles."

Liberty's voice dropped. "Don't get your

hopes up. Some miracles don't last forever, you know. Call me if I can be of any more help."

"Honey, you've done great. Thanks a thousand—I mean a million." Rita couldn't wait until her husband returned. She called her contact at the Department of Motor Vehicles and used their standard check system. It worked! The Blazer was registered to a Mr. and Mrs. John C. Christianson at 1225 No. Pull Street.

Rita filed and painted her long nails nervously as she waited for Collin. She fidgeted and folded three sticks of gum into her salivating mouth. An hour later her husband returned to the office, slumped and dejected. But when he peered through the window and saw the hot pink, lipsticked grin on his wife's face, he knew she'd had better luck. He slipped on the icy sidewalk twice before he finally made his way to the door. Rita's three-inch high heels didn't slow her down as she bustled toward him. She grabbed his coat collar and pulled him inside.

"I found him, Poopsy. I found Mr. Claus. His Christmas Blazer with 'I believe' license plates gave him away."

Each word she sputtered was more animated than the last, and her gum chomping and popping was so rapid that she looked like a frightened squirrel chewing an acorn.

"Let's call Doctor Thomas right now, Collin."

"Wait a second. This only took us . . ." He checked his watch and slowly removed his hat and coat. "If the good doctor thinks we only spent two and a half hours, he's not going to be happy about paying us all this money. Let's wait a while."

The two sat still for thirty minutes—as long as they could stand it. Collin grabbed the phone. Rita picked up the extension. Collin spoke. Dr. Thomas didn't answer. Collin tried his cellular number.

"Hello, this is Desmond Thomas."

"Hello, Doctor. This is Collin Mathers." Collin was breathing so heavily he had to cover the phone so he wouldn't sound too eager. "I have found," he glanced at Rita, "I mean, we have found Saint Nick."

"In three hours? You're a genius, Mathers. A genuine genius. Hold on, I'm pulling over."

Desmond was elated. He slid his red car to the curb and snatched a notepad and pen out of the glove box. "Okay, give me the name and address." He scribbled illegibly but was able to read it back to check its accuracy.

"That's it, Doc. Good luck. Thanks for the business, and if you ever need help again, remember us at the Lost and Found Detective Agency . . . "

"You lose 'em, we find 'em," Desmond completed the jingle. "You're the best! I'll recommend you to everyone I know, and I'll be back. Count on it. Merry Christmas, Mathers. Good-bye."

On his way to the address, Desmond called his attorney and asked him to run a quick check on a John Christianson. His attorney called him back almost immediately.

Having learned that John Christianson had served for several years as a district court judge, Dr. Thomas expected a lavish mansion but instead he encountered a well-maintained cottage, simple, warm, and inviting. The Christianson home was surrounded by a grove of ancient pine trees. Snowflakes from the previous evening's storm sifted through the trees, and the scene looked like a Christmas postcard. The walkways and driveway were freshly scraped, and large mounds of snow formed tunnels that surrounded the home. Not surprisingly, a bright red Chevrolet Blazer rested in the driveway. Desmond smiled when he saw the holly leaves and green pinstriping. *This guy really believes he's Santa Claus.* No sooner had Desmond slowed his sports car to a stop and hopped out in front of the Christianson home than a large, bearded man burst through the front door, chased by three young boys. Two of the boys were dressed as Indians, flinging toy arrows at the older man. The other boy was a cowboy with hat, chaps, and boots, and was shooting a cap gun in every direction. Upon seeing his visitor, the bearded man called out, "Take cover! Take cover! The cowboys and Indians have joined forces. They're coming." The larger man dived into a snowbank and pulled Desmond in after him.

Buried in the snow, Desmond extended his right hand. "Good morning, sir. I believe we have met on one previous occasion. My name is Dr. Desmond Robert Thomas." In his left hand, he still held Libby's Christmas tree ornament.

The larger man rolled over onto his belly, looked at Desmond's face, and smiled. "Ah, yes, I believe I've seen you on television, young man." John struggled to get his hand out from under himself and shook Desmond's right hand. "I recall that you donate your services to the poor and needy on Christmas Eve. Isn't that so? To what do I owe the pleasure of this visit, Dr. Thomas?"

By now, the cowboy and Indians had landed atop their energetic grandfather. Gesturing toward the house, the Honorable John Christianson begged mercy from his grandsons and promised to return quickly. The boys reluctantly released their prisoners, and Desmond and John stood and brushed the snow from themselves. As the two men walked silently toward the cottage, John removed his oversized holster and cowboy hat.

Ruth Christianson opened the front door, drying her hands on a dish towel and beginning to scold John. Then she spied Desmond standing on her porch. Immediately Desmond recognized her as the beggar woman that Santa had carried into the emergency room on Christmas Eve. Then, she was dressed as a beggar woman. Now, she was outfitted in charcoal-colored wool slacks and a beautiful green and white sweater depicting a Christmas tree with presents beneath it. Her silvery hair was shoulder length. She was stunning. Similarly, Judge Christianson was an impressive looking man. He stood nearly as tall as Desmond, with shoulders that were even more broad and sturdy. He had a healthy look with his ruddy, red complexion showing through his full white beard. Yes, indeed, Desmond knew he had found his Santa Claus.

Ruth's eyes sparkled, just as they had done on Christmas Eve when she had lightly patted Desmond's cheeks and thanked him for giving of himself by providing medical services to those in need. John and Ruth had secretly planned and orchestrated a Christmas Eve gathering to serve both Dr. Thomas and a number of indigent patients. At first, Dr. Thomas had been upset by the intrusion into his usually organized and sanitized emergency room. But when he realized that the hospital administration had authorized a local television reporter to record the incident, he had been pleased with Ruth's description of him as the doctor who gave freely to those in need on Christmas Eve. After the initial shock, Dr. Thomas had enthusiastically helped every patient, in particular, a tiny six-year-old girl named Anna. Her fractured arm paled in comparison to her obvious need for attention and love.

Desmond's mind wandered as Ruth led him through their home to a cozy study. Inside the room, Desmond noticed an eclectic collection of gathered memories. Certificates demonstrated John's prominence as a judge. A teaching certificate acknowledged the degree bestowed upon one Ruth Christianson. Pictures of children and grandchildren all smiled vividly at Desmond. On one side of the study sat a large, oak, roll-top desk. Opposite the desk was a fireplace, on one side of which was an overstuffed chair with an ottoman to match. Sitting on the ottoman was a Jefferson-style lap desk covered with papers and handwritten notes. On the other side of the fireplace was a dainty Queen Anne writing table holding a neat stack of papers and an antique gold fountain pen. The remaining walls were built-in bookshelves—a veritable library of fiction, law, and adventure.

John invited Desmond to sit at the roll-top desk, swiveling the chair around to face the fireplace. Ruth took her place at the Queen Anne desk, and John sat uncomfortably on the edge of the ottoman.

"Dr. Thomas, welcome to our home. I must say it is a great surprise to see you here." John spread his arms wide, and Desmond admired the immense stature of the man before him. "What can we do for you?" asked John.

Desmond's mind raced over his rehearsed speech. He had vowed not to discuss the Christmas Eve caper this couple had committed. Rather, he intended to focus upon his search for little Anna. But sitting here as he was, he couldn't resist asking the older couple what had possessed them to bring their Christmas gathering to his hospital, and why, of all the doctors in the city, they had focused their Christmas Eve visit upon him.

"You must know that I . . . ah . . . was completely surprised by your visit on Christmas Eve."

Ruth laughed. "I assure you, young man, everyone we visit on Christmas Eve is, to say the least, surprised. If it's about the cost of the care you gave the people, my husband and I will certainly pay for your time and your services." John scooted closer, nearly touching Desmond's knees.

Desmond looked back and forth from Ruth to John. He was embarrassed. "No, it's not that at all. I'm not here about the money. I came because of . . . because of the little girl. You see, I would like to see her again, but I have no idea how. His mind buzzed. So many questions swarmed inside his head. "And it would be very nice to know why, of all the doctors in the city, you two chose to visit me."

John and Ruth exchanged a cautious look. It was clear they knew something they had not been prepared to share. After an awkward pause, Ruth spoke first.

"Desmond, we know where you can find little Anna, and if it's help you want to give, we're more than happy to assist in that. But her feelings are quite fragile. She's been through a lot in her young life, and there is something you should know first. Our lives—John's, mine, and yours—are more intertwined than you may ever imagine. There's a story that you deserve to hear."

Ruth looked toward John to explain the mystery of how their visitor's life was joined to that of an old couple he'd never known until Christmas Eve, just two days before. John shifted uneasily under the weight of his wife's expectation. He looked at the flames glowing in the fireplace, and then at his wife. Finally he met Desmond's intensely questioning gaze.

"It's true, Desmond. Our paths have met on more than one occasion. In fact, Ruth and I learned of you and your family nearly two decades ago." John spoke slowly, carefully selecting his words.

"Long before you were born, we came to know a man, an exceptional man, a physician such as yourself, named Dr. Jesse Rose. Ruth and I had reached a point of despair in our world, but Dr. Rose healed our despair and showed us a better life. We were struggling students, working to survive and complete our education. On a cold Christmas Eve, more than forty years ago, Ruth ventured out of our apartment to make her way to the hospital to deliver our firstborn son. I was working. She was alone and lost in a snowstorm, but she was saved from the bitter cold by a group of homeless people. When I found my wife, she wore a gift of love on one hand—an old glove shared with her by a homeless woman."

"Mr. Christianson, I beg your pardon, but I have no idea how this has anything to do with me."

"All in good time, my boy. All in good time. On that Christmas Eve, when those homeless people took Ruth and cared for her in my absence, this kind and gentle man, Dr. Rose, safely delivered our son. Providence would have it that Dr. Rose was ministering to the homeless when he found my wife—also in need—among them. We named our son John Rose Christianson. He is the reporter who interviewed you for television on Christmas Eve."

A look of recognition crossed Desmond's face. He was impatient to learn what the homeless people had to do with him, how their lives were connected, and what it all meant. "So the reporter is your son? The entire visit to the hospital was a set-up?"

Ruth slid forward and answered Desmond directly. "No, it was no set-up. You see, we believe that things happen for a reason. We had wondered for years how we could bring Christmas back into your life."

Desmond looked at her in astonishment. *How could she know? How could she know that I had stopped believing?*

John began again where he had left off. His measured cadence emphasized every word. "If

Dr. Rose had not been caring for the homeless that night, I shudder to think what would have happened to my Ruthie." John held his wife's hand, and tears of love stung his eyes. Dr. Rose visited those in need on Christmas Eve every year until he died. That good doctor showed us how to celebrate the birth of Jesus and find happiness in following his example."

Ruth reached out and took Desmond's hand. "We can't give medical attention to the needy as Dr. Rose did, but over the years we have found many ways to gather Christmas. We believe that Santa Claus is real. He lives through those who anonymously give."

Desmond shook with anticipation. "But why me? Why . . . how . . . did you choose me?"

John squeezed Ruth's hand and sighed heavily. Ruth nodded for him to continue. "Dr. Rose was there the night you lost your father and sister. He found you in the hospital chapel, and he heard your prayer. It was he who gathered up your offering. He took only one of your gloves, and he left the other for you. Dr. Rose couldn't make your father and sister live, but he did respond to your father's last plea: 'Please, God, care for my wife and son!'"

John looked toward Ruth. Without hesitation, Ruth continued. "Dr. Rose followed your life. He saw great promise hidden beneath the struggling and bitter young boy you became. He vowed that his legacy of love would continue beyond his own life. Your father's prayer was answered through Dr. Rose. As you entered junior high school, Dr. Rose approached John and me. By this time, John was already serving as a circuit court judge and had established himself as a man of integrity. Dr. Rose knew my husband's reputation. You see, he also followed our lives after he delivered our son. He asked John to take responsibility for a sizable amount of money which was to be placed in a trust with Desmond Robert Thomas Jr. as the beneficiary. Each year on Christmas Eve we visited your home and gave your mother the next year's money inside a tattered glove. Of course, John was always dressed as Santa Claus, and I, as his beggar woman. To this day, your mother does not know the source of the money given her."

Desmond looked at the floor. "Oh yes she does. She knows that it came from Santa Claus. I remember. She told me many times that he is real. Every year when I wrote my letter to Santa, she told me to have faith and Santa would bring just what we needed. But I was angry when I didn't get what I asked for—the bike, the army set, the microscope—and I thought she lied to me about Santa. I refused to believe. But now I know she was right. Oh, Mother, can you ever forgive your bitter son? It—he—is real. I do believe." Desmond covered his face with his hands.

John and Ruth knelt beside him and embraced him. Ruth whispered, "Yes, Desmond. We, too, believe."

Desmond felt the arms of peace and love close softly around him. He felt a miracle, and he silently prayed for the feeling to live forever.

Extending

It was Desmond's favorite time of day. The sun had set behind the western mountains and now cast a pink and orange glow along the ridge lines, outlining individual evergreen trees with pale gleams of fading light. As darkness swallowed light, Desmond usually spent his time watching the city from his lofty Avenues windows. Instead, now he felt as if he were blindly racing against time. As he hastened down the back streets of the city's west side, the scattered street lights began to flicker. The west side was as colorless as the decor in his Avenues home. The gray streets lay enveloped in dirty snow blended with chain-link fences, broken glass, and gray slush. As he entered what was known as Homeless Haven, Desmond was surprised at the number of people actually on the streets. He'd expected the streets to be vacant, given the heavy snowfall and freezing temperatures. The entire scene that surrounded Desmond appeared much like an etched charcoal drawing—shapeless, cold, without passion.

As he identified the address for the shelter and its accompanying School with No Name, a flicker of concern flashed inside Desmond's mind. Where would he park his precious car? Then, with previously unknown abandon, Desmond found the first vacant spot at the curb and left his car in search of little Anna. He and his car contrasted starkly with the dismal surroundings. Homeless men huddled together, speaking in muffled tones. Small children clung to their parents' legs, and everyone swayed back and forth attempting to keep warm.

Standing taller than everyone around him, Desmond saw the metal-framed glass doors leading to the entry of the shelter. At last, he saw some color. Many of the people around him wore red mittens. He smiled when he thought of John and Ruth Christianson's selfless giving. Desmond found no knobs or handles on the doors. Two secure metal bars blocked the shelter entrance. Undaunted, he knocked loudly on the doors to get the attention of an attendant near the reception desk. The attendant seemed oblivious. Soon a group of homeless people swarmed around him. With some embarrassment, he finally noticed an intercom not far from the door frame. He pressed the button, and the small box crackled. "Yes, may I help you?"

"Yes, I, ah . . . this is Doctor Thomas. I've come to check up on the patients I treated on Christmas Eve. I need some additional information for my files."

The attendant suddenly seemed interested in the tall visitor standing outside the door. "All right, sir, I'll need to see some credentials, and then I can buzz you in."

Realizing that he had left his medical bag in his car, Dr. Thomas pressed his face closer to the glass doors. "Could you wait just one moment while I get my things?"

The attendant watched Dr. Thomas hurry through the gathering crowd outside the doors.

He found what appeared to be a flock of rav-
enous, predatory birds all perched atop his
precious car. Each ruffled coat and scarf con-
cealed an unwashed face. Many of these street
children wore wool caps, and all of their clothing carried the filth in which they lived.

"Hey! What are you doing there?"

Startled by the return of the car's owner,
the flock of bird children took flight in every
direction. The car that moments before had
never known a blemish, was covered with
slushy footprints and hand marks, and the
prized hood ornament was missing.
Desmond's first reaction was to pursue his car's
assailants. But then, he was comforted when
he saw Libby's ornament hanging from his
rear-view mirror. Realizing it would be futile
to chase hungry children through the streets
and remembering his commitment to change,
he returned to the task at hand with new re-
solve.

As he made his way back to the attendant,
his path was blocked by a few men and
women pushing shopping carts overflowing
with tattered odds and ends, pieces of cloth,
discarded household items, cardboard packag-
ing, and the remnants of what once had been
blankets. Plastic bags filled with aluminum
cans rattled and sang a discordant song of

poverty as the caravan sloshed through the street. Once again, Desmond noticed the conspicuous red woolen mittens.

Desmond held his leather medical satchel in one hand and pressed his wallet and medical license against the glass for the attendant to see.

"All right, Doctor Thomas. Come right in."

"Thank you. Where will I find the families living in this shelter?" He glanced back once more at the flock of bird children that had once again perched around and on top of his car, and then he followed the attendant.

They passed two large, hand-painted murals. Each mural depicted a happy scene with lush, green parks and children at play. Airplanes flew overhead, and joyful people joined hands in the idyllic scenes that in every way seemed out of place in this dismal shelter. Desmond noticed that the facility was surprisingly clean and orderly. He passed a kitchen with numerous refrigerators and stoves where some families had gathered to eat their evening meal. Next they passed the children's play area, which also appeared to function as a library.

Beyond the play area, Desmond heard excited voices. The attendant led him to a classroom filled with children. He surveyed the classroom with its aquarium, gerbil cages, assorted chalkboards, and bulletin board. In the middle of the room, an old three-man camping tent had been pitched and was surrounded by a group of desks. In a far corner of the classroom, a beautiful young woman was helping the students place pins in a map of the United States. Each pin was attached to a string that in turn was attached to a name card bearing the handwriting of its namesake. There was no mistaking the identity of the child sought by Desmond. There she stood, extending her arm in its cast to place a pin in the map.

The child seemed confused, perhaps a little frightened. She looked at her teacher for reassurance, and yet no answer was forthcoming. It was clear that no place on this map could be called Anna's home. The teacher stepped forward and guided Anna's tiny hand to the Rocky Mountains and helped her to sink the pin. At that very moment, the teacher observed Desmond's presence in the room. He raised his index finger to his lips, expressing his own contentment to await completion of the lesson.

With their classroom tasks finished, some of the children recognized Desmond as Dr. Thomas, the good doctor who had helped them on Christmas Eve. He patiently inspected each bandage, each suture, and finally the little girl with her arm in a cast. The other students stepped forward one at a time to have the doctor listen to their heart. Dr. Thomas found something kind to say to each child. Once he had pronounced good health upon each one, he turned to the teacher.

"Thank you for letting me take the time to follow up with my patients."

"No, it is I who am grateful to you for helping the children. It's not often that we get a house call directly to our School With No Name. Usually the people here wait in endless lines at city or county clinics and are typically seen by physicians' assistants or nurses, if at all."

"Well, there were a couple of acute cases I did want to see again after our visits at the hospital on Christmas Eve. For example, the little girl there with the cast on her arm. Can you tell me about her?"

"There really isn't much to tell, except that Anna won't be with us long. You see, Anna has no parents, and this facility is dedicated to "families" who are making progress toward reestablishing themselves in society. They want very much to be independent. But Anna is alone. You could say we have sort of adopted her while she is in transition to other care."

While Desmond talked to the teacher, parents retrieved their children from the class-room. Anna lingered behind. She sat beside the aquarium with her chin on the shelf, watching the fish and attempting to conceal her interest in the conversation between her teacher and Dr. Thomas.

"I'm concerned about the fracture on her arm, and I'd hoped to see her again. Would you mind if I spent some time just getting to know her?"

"No, not at all. Although I will warn you that Anna doesn't like to talk about herself. She's lived a troubled life, and I think the memories are too painful to discuss. So, she focuses on the present and not much more.

Desmond smiled at little Anna. He knew how she felt. Anna looked back at him blankly. He crunched himself into a small chair beside the aquarium and the child. He, too, rested his chin on the shelf. Neither spoke, they just watched the fish gliding through the water. After a while, the teacher left the room. Without raising her head, Anna's eyes followed the teacher to the door and then slowly focused on Desmond's right ear. Still neither of them spoke.

Finally, Anna's gruff voice broke the silence. "Did you know you have hair growing out of your ear?" She turned back to watch the scavenger fish suck rocks at the bottom of the aquarium.

Desmond smiled inside but showed no outward sign of amusement. He blinked a few times slowly and without lifting his chin or turning his head, he answered. "Yeah, I ate too much chocolate when I was a kid."

Anna still didn't turn or lift her head. Desmond reached inside his pocket and pulled out a chocolate bar. He watched the fish while he unwrapped the candy and broke off a few pieces. As he chewed, his jaw jerked his head up and down on the bookshelf. He situated the remaining chocolate on the space between his own chin and Anna's. Anna scanned the candy out of the corner of her eye. She smelled its sweetness, and her mouth immediately watered. Her small hand inched toward the chocolate. Then, in one quick movement, she snatched the treat and popped it into her mouth. She closed her eyes and savored the smooth chocolate as it melted on her tongue and slid down her throat. Desmond felt her enjoyment. He listened to her satisfied sigh. When he looked at her, she wore a smile.

"So, Anna Banana Roseanna Danna likes chocolate, does she?"

"I don't like it as much as I like you."

He was astonished at Anna's frankness. "You do?"

"Do what?"

"Like me?"

"Of course! Doesn't everybody? You help people and you share your chocolate and sometimes you smile. What's not to like?"

"I'm afraid I haven't always been very nice to people, Anna. And I'm sorry to say, I haven't been one to share much, either. As for smiles, until I met you, I had forgotten how to smile."

Anna finally shifted her focus from the aquarium. She peered at Desmond, and he looked back at her. "What a crock!" she said. People don't forget how to smile. They just quit trying."

"You're absolutely right, Anna. I quit trying. But now I'm trying again. See?" Desmond showed her his cheesiest grin.

"You look quite handsome when you smile."

"Where did you learn that word?"

"Handsome?"

"No, *crock*."

"Crock? Oh, my best friend says it a lot. It just means 'baloney' or 'phooey'—you know, something like that. Libby says it's a crock when I say I'll never get a family of my own.

She says it's a crock that I think my mom left me here alone because she didn't like me. Libby thinks lots of things are a crock ."

Desmond couldn't believe that Anna could be talking about Liberty Taylor. But there couldn't be more than one Libby who said crock a lot. "Tell me more about your friend Libby."

"Libby's the first real friend I ever had. She's fun. She smiles a lot, and she's real pretty. You should know her—she works at the same hospital you do. She just volunteers here twice a week on her time off. Should I tell you a secret about Libby?"

"Yes, please. I love secrets." Desmond was now certain that their two Libby's were one and the same, and he was anxious to know everything.

"Swear you won't tell anyone? Pinkie swear?"

Desmond had learned this ritual from another child he'd treated. He linked his pinkie finger with Anna's, they blinked their eyes three times, then they spit into the nearby trash can. Anna was thoroughly impressed that Dr. Thomas knew how to pinkie swear.

"I, Desmond Robert Thomas, swear never to tell anyone the secret Anna is about to tell me."

Anna was satisfied. "Okay. Come close, and I'll whisper in your ear." She stared at his ear for a moment and then commented with a small amount of disgust. "I don't think chocolate really does that."

"I suppose you think that's a crock, too. Don't you?"

"Yup." Anna yanked his ear close to her mouth. "Libby's in love."

"How do you know that?" Desmond was concerned, and Anna read his expression.

"Don't worry. Libby says he's a good person. She says he's a doctor that she works with. She says he doesn't even know that she loves him. Isn't that romantic?"

Desmond perked up. "A doctor? What kind of a doctor?"

"A good one. Libby would only love a good doctor, I'm sure. Libby says he has big, strong hands." Desmond glanced at his hands. "And she says that he's tall and . . ."

"Handsome?" Desmond asked, grinning. He was recalling how Libby had arranged her schedule to work almost every shift with him the last few months, and how she had invested so much time in trying to convince him that life is good, and how she had so eagerly accepted his invitation to Christmas brunch.

"No, she didn't say handsome. What was it

she said?" Anna put her thumbnail between her teeth and gnawed at it. "Oh, yeah. She said he's tall and mi-zer-lee."

Desmond slumped on his little chair and almost tipped it over. Once again, Anna sensed his concern.

"Don't worry. Libby said she could help him."

Desmond smiled a wounded smile and sat up straighter.

"What is mi-zer-lee, anyways?"

"Miserly is . . . well . . . a tendency to be unable to part with one's money."

"You mean even if you have it, you still can't spend it?"

"Especially if you have it. Seems the more you have, the worse it gets."

"So, it's a disease?"

"No, not really. It's kind of a game . . . a challenge. You get some money, and then you challenge yourself to see how much of it you can save. If you spend it, you lose. But if you save it, you win."

"What do you win?"

"Well, you win financial security, interest on the money you save, self-discipline . . . ."

"That's a crock. If I had lots of money, I'd spend it." Anna looked at Desmond respectfully. "Okay. I'd save a little, but I'd spend most of it. I'd buy Libby a new dress with shoes to match, and I'd buy you a candy bar. I'd buy Teacher a book like Treasure Island, and I'd buy all of the kids in my school their own crayons. I'd make everyone so happy." Then Anna looked at the floor. "But Libby says that money can never buy happiness, and I know she's right because after she told me that, I was thinking—you can't just go to a store, walk up to the lady, hold out your dime, and say, 'I'd like ten cents' worth of happiness, please.' She wouldn't know what to give you, now would she? Libby says she'd rather have love than money. But she's afraid her doctor would rather have money than love."

"Did she say that?"

"No, that's just what I think she thinks. Now me, I'd be perfectly happy with just a little of both." Anna smiled and winked at Desmond.

Desmond returned her wink. His breathing accelerated with excitement as he inhaled the thought that Libby had as much as admitted her love for him to Anna. He remembered Libby's words, *My favorite pastime at Christmas is spending money—frivolously.* He laughed out loud, jumped to his feet, picked up Anna, and raced out the door with her. They met Anna's teacher in the hallway next to the colorful mural.

"Miss Stacie, could I please take Anna with me just for a little while?" Desmond panted. "I'll have her back by suppertime."

Anna grinned at the thought of being with Desmond. "It's okay, Miss Stacie. He's a friend of Miss Libby. He works at the hospital with her."

"Well, this isn't our usual policy." Miss Stacie frowned. "You'd have to sign her out. Come with me." They walked to the front desk. "We have all of your credentials from your check-in today, don't we, Doctor?"

"Yes you do, Miss Stacie." Desmond was being as charming as he knew how.

"And you're a friend of Liberty Taylor?" She looked him over carefully.

"Yes. I am her friend," he chuckled. He wanted to shout that he was much more than her friend, that she actually loved him, but he restrained himself for the time being.

"Very well. Any friend of Libby's is a friend of ours. You may go, Anna, but you behave yourself."

"I assure you, Miss Stacie, I'll take very good care of this child."

"Oh, I'm not worried about Anna, Doctor. She can take care of herself. It's you I'm concerned for. Anna has a way of stealing hearts."

Miss Stacie kissed Anna's cheek and hurried off for the child's coat.

Desmond knelt down to put her in it. "Where are we going, Dr. Thomas?"

"We are going to spend some money—frivolously."

"What does *frivolously* mean?"

"It means just for fun—without even keeping track of how much we've spent."

"Wow! I've never done this before."

"Me neither, Anna. Me neither." Desmond tied her hood under her chin, and they hurried through the slush to his waiting car. Once inside, Anna grinned and began to sing softly, "Jingle bells, jingle bells. Jingle all the way . . . " Desmond joined in much more loudly and much less on tune. Libby's tree ornament swayed to the beat. "Oh what fun it is to ride . . . " They sang and drove as they began their adventure together.

Anna leaned her head back against the seat back and inhaled a deep breath of new leather. She was elated. She closed her eyes and peacefully dreamed that this feeling would live forever.

Venturing

Desmond drove more carefully than usual. He glanced at Anna. She was drawing pictures on the frosty window with her finger. Remembering how he used to do the same thing added warmth to his heart.

"Could you turn on the radio, please, Dr. Thomas? I like music."

"I'll turn it on if you promise not to call me Dr. Thomas anymore."

"Okay. What should I call you?"

"What would you like to call me?"

"I dunno. Let's see. How about I call you Des? That's short for Desmond."

"Des it is. How about I call you Anna Banana Roseanna Danna? That's long for Anna." He emphasized the "Rose." They exchanged smiles, and Anna whispered, "I love roses. They smell pretty, and they look pretty, too."

Desmond slowed to a stop in front of a small women's clothing boutique. Elegant gold lettering spanned the white stucco above the huge gold-framed glass doors. *Char's Closet,* pronounced as if the Ch were an Sh, was quite obviously the perfect place for frivolous money spending.

"Well, Anna Roseanna, I like roses, too. It's been a long time since I thought about flowers, but now I remember just how much I like them. Do you know what? You remind me of a beautiful red rose, and roses make me think of all that's good in life. I'll have to tell you a story about a wonderful man named Dr. Rose, and a chapel door made of roses, and someone I once loved named Lizzy. Oh, too much to tell in such a short time. We'll have plenty of time for stories later. Right now, we've got to rid ourselves of some money. You ready?"

"To go in that store?" Anna pointed to

Char's Closet and her eyes grew two sizes. "I'm ready if you are, Des." They hurried out of the car and into the shop. A tall brunette woman met them at the door and took their coats. Another tall woman, this one blonde, greeted them and spoke in a smooth, low voice.

"Hello. Welcome to *Char's Closet*. You two look as if you could use a warm drink. We have *Stephen's Gourmet White Cocoa*, or we have hot wassail." Then she leaned down to speak to Anna. "Which would you prefer, sweetheart?"

The woman seemed gigantic to the small child, and Anna moved behind Desmond, pretending not to hear. Desmond sensed Anna's fear and spoke for her. "We both prefer the white cocoa, please." Anna slipped her hand into his as the blonde, giant woman left to get their chocolate.

"Thanks, Des," Anna whispered. "She makes me sort of nervous."

"She makes me nervous, too." He smiled as the woman returned and handed them each a full teacup on a small saucer. The cups were white with gold rims, and the saucers were the same. Desmond and Anna sat down in two tall-backed white chairs to enjoy their white chocolate.

"This place is real clean, isn't it, Des?" Anna gazed at the walls.

"Sure is. Everything's white—carpet, curtains, chairs, walls, even the cocoa." Then he whispered, "I feel like I'm in a hospital."

Anna laughed. She smelled the cinnamon pot pourri. "Yeah, except it smells a lot nicer here."

"You got me there. What do you say we get on with this spending thing?"

"I'm ready. How do we do it?"

"I'm not really sure. I guess we'll find out." Desmond motioned the tall brunette over to him and talked with her. "We'd like something pretty—a dress, please."

"With shoes to match," Anna added, bolder than before.

"My name is Alicia, and I'll help you find exactly what you want. Is this a gift?" The tall lady seemed as if she sincerely wanted to help them, and Anna was liking her more.

"Yes," Desmond and Anna answered in unison.

"For your mother, I'll bet." The lady smiled toward Anna. Anna's brow furrowed and she started to explain, but Desmond interrupted.

"We need something gorgeous for Mother, don't we, Anna?" Desmond winked overzealously so Anna would catch on. Anna knew at once that they were pretending. She was thrilled to act as if Desmond were her father, and together they were buying a gift for her mother.

"Oh yes, Mother deserves the very best. She's so good to us all."

"All?" Alicia questioned.

"Of course. I have . . . uh . . . six brothers and . . . uh . . . three sisters. That makes . . . um . . ." Anna hurried a count on her fingers— "ten children. With Mom and Dad, we make twelve." Anna ended with a satisfied nod.

The woman looked at Desmond horrified. He smiled. "An even dozen. It's convenient, don't you think?"

"For what?" the woman asked, mostly under her breath. "Egg buying?"

Anna and Desmond pretended not to hear, and the woman said she'd be right back with some ideas for them.

The two inexperienced shoppers rested patiently, listening to Bing Crosby's rendition of "I'm Dreaming of a White Christmas" sounding softly over the store's stereo system. Anna said she'd never seen a white Christmas tree, and Desmond explained that the store's tree had flocking on it to look like snow. Anna especially liked the little gold tree ornaments that hung all over the tree. They glittered in the white lights.

"What a crock. Nobody's going to believe

that tree has snow on it in here. Anybody knows it would have melted by now."

Desmond laughed. He liked seeing his smile in the beveled mirror beside the fireplace. He liked what he felt, and he loved being with Anna. The tall Alicia appeared and asked what size dress and shoes they needed. Desmond guessed at the size, making certain they could be exchanged if necessary.

A procession of tall models paraded by, one after another, for Desmond and Anna to choose a dress. With each one, Anna oohed and aahed at the lovely clothing and the women. Finally, a not-so-tall auburn-haired model came out from behind the curtain. She wore a simple cream-colored dress with pearl earrings and shoes to match. Anna thought it was the most elegant, so Desmond stopped the show.

"We'll take that one. Shoes and earrings as well."

"Oh, Mother will be stunning in that outfit," Anna gawked.

Alicia assured them, while she wrapped, that they had made a good choice. "Your mother will love this. Imagine! Ten children and she still wears a size 8. Wow!"

"Hard to believe, isn't it?" Desmond shrugged. Once outside the store the two charaders burst into uncontrolled laughter. They jumped inside Desmond's car and sped away.

"That was fun, Des. I like being frivolous."

"So do I, Partner, so do I."

Desmond chauffeured Anna through the avenues to his house. Anna liked his house, but she strongly suggested that he needed some Christmas decorations.

"That's funny. That's what Libby said when she came here."

"Libby's been here, too?" Anna asked incredulously. "So, who's the lucky lady that gets the dress?"

Desmond was afraid to tell Anna that the dress was actually for Libby. He didn't want her to share his secret with Libby as she'd shared Libby's with him, so he attempted to satisfy the child with a white lie.

"You wouldn't know her."

"What's her name?" Anna followed him through each room, persisting. Finally, recalling a name on one of the tags he'd seen at the store, he answered. "Liz—uh—Liz Claiborne. You'll like her a lot."

"Well, I don't know, Des. Does she smile a lot like Libby?"

"She sure does." They walked out through Desmond's front door and down the long row of steps to Desmond's car.

"Is she nice and friendly like Libby?" Anna

continued her questions as they drove toward the shelter.

"She is that, too. In fact, she's a whole lot like Libby. I have one more gift to pick up. It's a small item, and the most expensive—I mean, the most important."

"Is it an engagement ring?"

"Now, how in the world would you know that?" Desmond was startled, but he didn't see any harm in telling Anna as long as she didn't know it was really Libby he intended to become engaged to, so he answered honestly. "Yes, it is an engagement ring, Anna. I'm going to beg her to marry me."

"Wow! That's so romantic. I wish I could be there to see Liz Claiborne's face when you ask her to marry you." Desmond laughed again.

"We're here, Anna Roseanna. Home, sweet home." Desmond needed to hurry to get the ring before the shop closed, so he and Anna scurried into the shelter. Anna thanked him, and he kissed her cheek.

"See you tomorrow, Anna."

"Really? You'll come back?"

"Nothing could keep me away, I promise." And Desmond hurried off to work his plan.

Later he stumbled through his back door. Two of the brightly wrapped packages on top of the stack that he bore in one arm slid off and fell to the floor. Luckily, they were unbreakable, the dress and shoes purchased from *Char's Closet.* He hoped they were the right size, but he couldn't be sure. He had never done anything like this in his life. *Who could imagine Dr. Desmond Robert Thomas on a shopping spree?* Well, perhaps some could think him capable of capitalizing on the after-Christmas sales. Nevertheless, it was an oddity for him to be carrying packages wrapped in, of all things, Christmas paper.

Desmond stomped the snow from his feet. He had experienced the frivolous shopping that Libby had convinced him she was accustomed to enjoying during her own Christmas holiday. Next, he dropped the small Christmas tree he had taken at a bargain from a local tree lot. Finally, he unloaded two packages tied carefully together. The first was rather large and heavy. Desmond smiled at it. Attached to the large package was a small, almost unnoticeable, box wrapped in elegant red foil paper and trimmed with red and green ribbon.

"Now for the decorations," Desmond said aloud. He removed an old box from the bottom drawer of his file cabinet. Upon opening the lid, he rediscovered a delightful assortment of handcrafted ornaments, each carefully carved from wood. Among them he found his favorite Christmas tree ornament carved from pine, and a beautiful flat Santa with a long, delicate beard. He hung the Santa near the base of the tiny Christmas tree. Next, he retrieved a six-cornered star in the shape of two intermingled triangles. He also found a shepherd's crook, a reindeer with long, fragile antlers, and finally a carving that depicted the Holy Family. In the bottom of the box he found one lonely green glove, the one he had offered in the hospital chapel long ago. The ornaments were the ones he had placed on the Stephenson tree. Mrs. Stephenson had taken them with her when she had gone to live with him and his mother after Mr. Stephenson, Lizzy, and Mr. Thomas had all died.

A few years earlier, Desmond had looked at the ornaments and the glove but had quickly boxed them back up when he'd started re-membering. Now he smiled at each one and yearned to recall every detail. He hung them all on the small tree. Then he placed Libby's gift-ornament on the top bough. He knew he needed to remember how to celebrate Christmas if he were going to start his own family.

At the shelter, Anna climbed into a worn-out pink nightie and smaller-than-twin bed. Alone in her closet-sized room, she strained to listen to the music in the hallway so that she didn't have to think about her past or her future. She left the door open just a crack so she could have some light. Though she hadn't prayed in a long time, she slipped out of bed onto the cold tile floor without noticing Libby's shadow at her door. Libby listened to Anna's soft words:

"Dear God—I didn't talk to you for a while and I'm sorry for that, but I just didn't have anything to say—that is until now. Before, all I had was me, and I figured it was pretty selfish to keep on praying for myself. But now I have someone else to pray for. I have a friend—'course you already know that, don't you, God? Well, anyways, my friend is Libby. She's in love with a good doctor—at least I think he must be a good one, 'cuz she'd never love a lousy doctor—but he doesn't know she loves him."

Libby smiled and wiped her tears. Anna continued:

"Libby loves him, so please help him love her back." Libby reached for the door but stopped when Anna's voice continued. "And as for my other friend, Dr. Thomas . . ." Libby was stunned. *Anna must remember Dr. Thomas from Christmas Eve.* "You know who I mean— Des. Well, he told me today that he's going to beg some lady named Liz that he used to love a long time ago to marry him." Libby gasped. "He even bought an engagement ring for her and everything. Could you please get her to say yes? I can tell by the way he acts that he loves her gobs and gobs. Thank you, God. That's all."

Anna thought she heard someone outside her door as she climbed back into bed. But she saw no one, so she closed her eyes and drifted away with the music.

Libby sneaked quietly away from Anna's door, trying to control her emotions, at least until she passed the attendant at the front desk. She had come to sneak a peek at Anna and maybe tuck her in. But though the first half of Anna's prayer tugged at Libby's heart, the second half broke it wide open. Libby jumped into her Toyota and cried all the way home.

Gran was in bed, but not yet asleep. Libby knocked softly.

"Come in, Liberty. I'm just reading."

Libby fell on the foot of Gran's bed, and Gran rested her book on her stomach. "What's happened, child?" She was alarmed at Libby's ashen face.

"Oh, Gran—no wonder he didn't call. Desmond's in love with another woman. I am so naive to have thought he was interested in me."

"Wait a minute, Liberty." Gran was somewhat relieved, knowing that her granddaughter would not die from a broken heart, but she had never seen Libby so upset.

"How can you be sure he's in love with someone else, dear?" Gran stretched her hand toward Libby. Libby took the wrinkled offering, hoping to let Gran remove some of the hurt. But the ache in Libby's heart worsened as she explained Anna's prayer. Gran and Libby talked most of the night. When the sun came up, Gran went to the kitchen and found Libby already there.

"I'm leaving, Gran. I've made up my mind. I can't keep working with Desmond knowing he loves someone else. You know the opening at the small hospital about forty-five miles south of here that I mentioned a while ago?"

"I remember, dear."

"Well, I'm going to take it—for a while at least. I called this morning. It's still available, and I'm going now for the interview." Libby was dressed and ready. Gran offered her a lemon poppy seed muffin before she left, but Libby refused.

"Gran, I just can't. It's too painful."

"Since when did my muffins become painful?"

"You know what I mean. I just can't discuss it."

"Very well," Gran sighed. "I'll see you this evening." Libby rushed out the door. The small hospital had pretty much assured Libby that she could have the position, so on her way she dropped off her letter of resignation at Valley Hospital—effective immediately.

———

Desmond whistled as he showered, shaved, and dressed. He was headed to Gran's house to find Libby. He knew where she lived because he'd secretly followed her home once or twice, trying to work up enough courage to talk to her. He also knew she lived with Gran because Anna had told him all about Gran. Anna had described Gran so well that Desmond could hardly wait to meet her.

He stopped his red car in front of the house, took a deep breath, and ran to the door. He rang the bell—twice. Gran answered.

"Yes, young man? What can I do for you?"

Desmond was carrying the large and small packages for Libby. Gran smiled, and

Desmond extended his hand. Gran immediately noticed the scar and knew from Libby's description who he was. Her smile left. She pursed her lips and squinted her eyes.

"So, you are Dr. Thomas."

"And you must be Gran. I've heard a lot about you."

"And I—you. What do you want?"

She peered into his eyes, and Desmond did not see the nice little old lady Anna had described, although she opened the door and reluctantly let him in. Desmond set the packages close to him, and Gran offered him a stale store-bought cookie with a glass of lukewarm water.

"My granddaughter is not here. She has gone out."

Desmond politely ate his dry cookie and took a swallow of water. He was thoroughly uncomfortable. He picked up the packages and left quickly, asking Gran to please tell Libby that he'd stopped by. Desmond raced to the hospital to see if Libby was there. He was devastated when he discovered her resignation. *Where would she have gone?* She had left no information at the hospital about where she'd gone, and she had told Susan, one of her nurse friends, that she did not want to be found— ever. Desmond could not figure out what was happening. He was so afraid that he had lost her forever.

"Collin Mathers. He's my only hope." Desmond was talking frantically to himself. He raced to the Lost and Found Detective Agency. He burst through the door. "Another thousand bucks if you can find my nurse, I mean, my friend, Liberty Taylor."

Collin was confused. "Doesn't she work with you at the hospital?"

"She used to. She quit, and now you've got to find her for me."

"Answer some questions for me. First, does she have any known relatives?"

"One that I know of, but she's not talking." He gave Collin Gran's name and number.

"Second, why do you want to find her?"

Desmond ran to the car and retrieved the gifts, the large one and the small one, and set them on Collin's desk. "I've got to give her these presents. She thinks I don't do Christmas, but now I do because now I believe." Desmond looked at Collin pleadingly. "Will you find her, please?"

"We'll do our best," Collin promised as Desmond gave him half the money.

But Desmond himself discovered Libby's whereabouts while he was attempting to enjoy his memory of Libby. He suddenly remembered her mentioning a head nurse job at a small hospital to the south. She had said she'd love to work in a small hospital—maybe make a real difference. That had to be it! Desmond raced to *Valley Hospital* and retrieved the name and address of the small hospital. At last he knew where he was going. He stopped to make one phone call to his mother. He also swung by the shelter school. Then he headed out to find Libby. Desmond was thrilled, and he finally believed that the feeling could live forever.

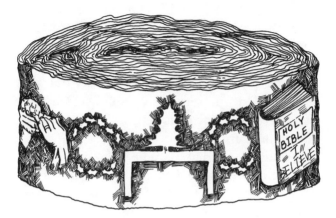

Embracing

Rita Mathers's gum popped as she chewed and talked. "Why didn't we just take this stuff to his house and dump it off there? We shouldn't have to drive in the snow all the way out here to the sticks to give it to him. It's not our fault he forgot his packages at our office. I mean, after all, we really did this guy a favor by finding his nurse friend."

Collin Mathers frowned at his wife, who

was holding a small box and a large cylinder-shaped package, both wrapped in red foil Christmas paper. "I can think of about two thousand reasons we ought to hand deliver these to him. Besides, we'll be there any minute. It's just a good thing for us that this guy needed our services again. The least we can do for the doctor is return the presents he left in our office."

Collin looked at his wife, who clearly hadn't heard a thing he'd said. She was using one of her inordinately long fingernails to peel away the tape on the wrapping paper so she could examine the contents of the packages. "Hey, what are you doing? You can't open that."

Rita looked up, rubbing her lips together to smooth out the heavy coatings of lipstick. "It won't hurt a thing for us to know what's in here. Besides, what if it's a bomb, and we're driving around with it in our van—wouldn't you like to know about that?"

"No, I would not like to know that. That package is private, and you shouldn't look in it. Now, put it down and leave it alone."

"That's my point. This thing is 'private' and we're private investigators. So we should look at it to see what it is." Rita popped her gum and continued removing the wrapping.

Collin reached for his wife's arm, momentarily losing control of the steering. The Mathers van lurched sideways and spun toward the side of the road. "Hold on!" Collin yelled as their van rolled onto the shoulder and careened into a clump of pine trees. Rita found herself on top of her husband. Both were covered with the scattered contents of the cluttered van. Rita's high-pitched scream could be heard for miles.

"My nail, you've broken my nail—I can't believe you broke my nail." Then she looked at her husband. "Oh, honey have you broken something, too?"

Collin was writhing in pain. "I'm sorry about your nail, but I can't move my left arm. I think it's broken." His arm hung limp from his shoulder, and he passed out.

———•••———

Desmond cautiously approached the entrance to the new emergency room of the Coalville General Hospital. Twenty-six years earlier he had abandoned any hope for happiness in this very place. Losing both his father and his sister to a senseless accident had caused a bitterness and a hatred for life that had metastasized in his heart and spread until it infected his entire soul. Ironically, amidst his own incurable bitterness, he had developed a determination to heal others. Years ago, as a helpless child yearning for someone to heal his dying father, he had vowed he would prevent others from suffering as his father had. Now, as an emergency room physician, he was fulfilling his promise. But, he had been unable to heal himself.

The automatic glass doors slid smoothly open when the motion detectors sensed Desmond's presence. He noted the significant change from the night he had been brought in here as a boy. Back then, he had waited for someone to respond to a simple doorbell that had summoned an on-duty nurse. Time had changed everything. Inside, one doctor and two nurses moved efficiently from patient to patient. Four people sat in a well-furnished reception area. A tall man nervously paced back and forth, blocking Desmond's view of a large aquarium. Now there was actually an emergency room. Trained emergency health care professionals were on duty. The equipment represented a conscious effort to modernize. Desmond was pleased and impressed.

After inspecting the surroundings, Desmond rested his scarred right hand on the reception desk and stared intently at the old wound—and then into his memory. He could still see the rose-petal doors and the stained glass windows of the hospital chapel. Desmond's jaw clenched and his muscles tightened as his memory joined him.

His father's hand stretched out to touch him. He heard his father's words, "Everything happens for a reason." His hand throbbed with pain from the deep wound, and yet that seemed unimportant as his father's life slipped away. If only he could have done something. If only he had then possessed the knowledge that was his now.

"Why couldn't I have done something? I was so helpless," Desmond muttered to himself.

"Excuse me, sir. What did you say? Sir? May I help you, sir?" a middle-aged woman with curly blonde hair questioned. She simply smiled until Desmond noticed her standing before him.

"Oh, excuse me. You caught me remembering. I, uh, can you tell me if there is a nurse who just started working here? Her name is Liberty Taylor. I've got to find her."

Skeptical of the tall, daydreaming visitor, the receptionist furrowed her brow. "I know that we are expecting a new head nurse here, but I don't know her name. Perhaps you could go to the main hospital registration area—they can give you more information there. Go up the stairs and to the right beyond our little chapel. You can't miss it. It's the second room past the fancy wooden door at the end of the hall."

Desmond nodded and turned toward the corridor. He hoped he could find what he had lost here so long ago. He attacked the stairs, three at a time. He reached the top and found the door, exactly as it had been. Warm light shafts beamed through the window and cast petal-shaped colored shadows onto the floor. He moved more slowly now, reverently. He looked back toward the emergency room then paused before approaching the rose-petal entry. A small brass plaque stated simply: "Chapel donated and woodwork hand-carved by Dr. J. Rose. Like his life, he dedicated this room to the healing of souls." Desmond felt so strange. Hope and commitment were pumping through his veins. He spoke softly. "What if my plan doesn't work? What if Libby won't have me? That would be the final—the ultimate loss." Desmond couldn't bear to experience devastation again. He had to convince Libby of his love and somehow capture her heart. He leaned against the beautifully carved wooden door and gathered his courage.

John and Ruth Christianson conversed
with Mrs. Thomas as they drove to the
Coalville General Hospital. They had sought
out Mrs. Thomas in the hope that she could
help them find her son. It was absolutely im-
perative that they find him so that he could ex-
ecute the necessary papers that John had prepared for Desmond to legally assume
guardianship and conservatorship responsibil-
ities for a young homeless girl. The deadline
for submission of the necessary documents
was December thirty-first. The end of the year
was fast approaching. He was to have met John
and Ruth at the courthouse, but he had left a
cryptic message for them that he "finally knew
what he needed to do" and he was "returning
to where he had lost his past so he could find
his future."

Mrs. Thomas was shocked as John and
Ruth reported the changes in her son, but she
admitted that she had received a strange call
from him in which he had testified that he
finally "believed in Santa and wanted to wish
her a belated merry Christmas." He had also
informed her that he had a surprise for her.

When Mrs. Thomas got the call from John and Ruth, she knew immediately where to find her son. She eagerly agreed to accompany John and Ruth to the hospital. Ruth had just reminded John to slow down because of the ice only moments before they witnessed the accident. The van in front of them whirled on the slippery road and then hit a patch of dry asphalt. It crashed against a large oak tree. While Ruth called for emergency assistance on their cellular phone, John immediately slowed the Blazer to a stop and jumped out to help. As he approached the overturned van, a slender young woman emerged from the passenger door, clutching what appeared to be a tree stump under one arm.

"Oh, thank heavens someone's here. Please help my husband—I think his arm is broken." Rita Mathers hobbled toward John and the red Christmas Blazer, each step piercing a spiked heel into the snow. John helped Rita to the Blazer, which Rita couldn't help noticing had green stripes and holly leaves painted on the sides.

"You're him! You're Santa Claus!"

John turned back toward the woman as he hurried to help her husband. He tried to quiet the hysterical woman. "How could you posslbly know that? Never mind. First we help your husband; then we'll talk."

The ambulance arrived within three minutes, and the attendants helped John remove Collin from the mangled van. "Thanks for your help, sir. We'll have this guy to the hospital in no time. It's just around the corner. Maybe you could follow us and bring his wife." The paramedic gestured toward Rita, who was screeching that she had to be with her husband.

"Yes, of course. We'll be right behind you."

"Where did you get this carved tree stump?" Mrs. Thomas firmly questioned Rita. The screaming halted abruptly. "Oh, it's not mine; it belongs to a doctor friend of ours. When he left it at our office, I demanded that my husband help me return it by hand delivery since it's a late Christmas gift for his nurse friend and all. The wrapping paper must have been torn off in the accident."

"May I see it?" Mrs. Thomas asked as she gently removed Desmond's evergreen miracle from Rita's lap and shifted it to her own. "I've never actually seen it before, but I would know these carvings anywhere. Desmond told me so much about them."

Rita's mouth hung open. "You know the doc, too?"

"I ought to—he's my son," Mrs. Thomas responded. Her words trailed off, and she examined the carvings. She saw the little hand-carved tree just as it had rested on the old Stephenson table. She read aloud her daughter's oath "I believe." As she examined the remaining carvings, she realized what they meant. She knew what her surprise was to be. As Mrs. Thomas closed her eyes, one more tear escaped and cascaded onto the wood. Just then the Christmas Blazer arrived at the hospital, and chaos erupted in the center of the peace that Mrs. Thomas felt. She hugged the evergreen miracle to her heart.

———

Desmond stood at the door of the chapel and placed his hands on the window. It was as warm as he remembered. Then he heard a commotion at the end of the corridor. A paramedic rushed past him to the chapel door.

"Ms. Taylor, come quick. We just got a call that an ambulance is on its way in with a car accident injury—a van rollover. They're on their way here now. We need all the help we can get."

Inside the chapel Desmond saw Libby sitting with Gran. Libby's eyes were red and swollen. Gran sat facing Libby, holding her hands. When Libby met Desmond's gaze, he noted a mixture of wonder and anger.

"What are you doing here?" Libby demanded.

"I came to find you. I had a gift for you, but I've lost it. Anyway that doesn't matter— I mean, I have to tell you something."

"Not now. There are people who need help. Come on." Libby pushed her way past him and started toward the emergency room.

"What I need to tell you cannot wait another minute." Desmond grasped her arm and turned her toward him. Gran stepped between them, wagging a slender index finger in Desmond's face and breaking his hold on her granddaughter.

"Listen here, Dr. Thomas. I don't want you doing anything more to break this young girl's heart. Rest assured that if you do anything to cause her more unhappiness, you'll have to contend with me, young man." Desmond turned back to Libby, but she was already bounding down the stairs and into the emergency room where she found none other than John and Ruth Christianson, Desmond's mother, and Rita Mathers. Desmond's mother cradled the precious carved pine in her arms.

Desmond followed Libby into the emergency room. "Mom—John, Ruth—what are you all doing here? Rita, what's going on?" Desmond stammered. He recognized Collin being wheeled into the emergency room by the paramedics. He didn't wait for an answer. Instead, he went to work assessing Collin's vital signs. Libby anticipated Desmond's every move. There was no question that the two had worked together before. The hospital's staff simply stood back and cleared the way for them. Libby started an IV line while Desmond placed a sheet around Collin's chest. He examined Collin, and the patient started to regain consciousness.

"Hey, Dr. Thomas. Is that you?" Collin groaned and reached for his client's arm.

"Try to hold still. I believe you may have a concussion, and your left arm has been dislocated. Of course, the dislocation we can attend to immediately." Libby pulled on the sheet while Desmond aligned himself and prepared to reset the arm. Libby tightened the tension on the sheet and Desmond pulled on the dislocated arm until, with one fluid motion, the arm was back in place.

"Ohhhhh! That smarts!" Collin was fully awake now and writhed with pain. Despite his own agony, he mustered the strength to explain why he and his wife had come looking for their favorite client. "We brought the gifts you left in our office. We knew they must be important, especially when you had us track down your nurse friend all the way out here. I thought the gifts were for her, but you left in such a hurry we couldn't catch you. We wrecked on the way because Rita was trying to . . . ."

"I was trying to get Collin to speed up. He always drives so slow. I just knew we needed to get these presents here *pronto*, but Collin lost control of the car, and you know the rest. Here's the little present. The big one must have gotten unwrapped in the accident." Rita approached Desmond and placed the small package in his outstretched hand.

Almost simultaneously, Desmond's mother stepped forward. "Son, I know what these carvings mean to you. Don't waste any more of your life on bitterness. I love you." She handed the pine tree stump to Desmond and kissed him on the cheek. Then she turned the evergreen miracle on its side to reveal a carving of three hands linked together. A woman's hand and a child's hand resting on a scarred, over-sized hand.

Libby stood looking back and forth at each person and each new revelation about Desmond. She thought she had lost him forever. She'd tried to convince herself that a new life away from him was best. And yet here he was with the evergreen carving he had so curiously introduced to her when she had visited his home. *What is he up to now?* she thought.

Desmond moved toward Libby, holding the carving in one hand and the small package in the other. "All of the most important events of my life are carved on this pine tree stump. Only one has yet to come true. Desmond dropped to one knee and offered her the small package.

"It seems as though I have known you for a lifetime. I treasure the time that we have worked together this past year. I have watched you care for God's children, young and old. I have seen your patience with the poor, the drunken, and the downcast. Most of all, I have felt your undying hope for me. And even though I'm sure it never showed, I have learned from your lessons of kindness. I love you, Libby."

He paused, and Libby accepted the package, afraid and yet eager to know its contents. The bright foil wrapping paper glistened as it fell to the floor. Libby opened the black velvet container. A sparkling diamond solitaire caught the light and reflected it in falls of blue and green light. Libby cried and smiled at once.

"I know this seems awfully sudden, but if you will have me, I would like you to be my wife. I love you for who you are and who you make me want to be. I've loved you for a long time, but when you insisted that Santa Claus is real, I knew I wanted to marry you. I need someone strong. I want to be strong for you, for us. And I want to share forever with you." Desmond finished the speech he'd been preparing in his mind for days. He reached out his scarred right hand and placed hers on top of his, just as it appeared in the carving. "Will you have me?"

Everyone in the emergency room had gathered around them—even a patient who was holding onto his IV pole leaned in to hear Libby's response. John and Ruth held each other tightly, and Desmond's mother stood close by in anxious anticipation. Gran stood next to Libby, hardly able to contain herself. Rita Mathers swallowed her gum.

After an uncomfortable silence, Desmond spoke again. "I wanted someone else to be here when I asked you to marry me, but when I went to get her, she was gone. They wouldn't tell me where. They said they had strict instructions from the person who took her, not to tell anyone where they'd gone. She's . . ."

"Anna? My little Anna from the shelter

school? Hers is the other hand in the carving, isn't it? Libby whispered.

"Yes."

"But she told me you were in love with someone named Liz. A woman that you loved a long time ago."

"Liz is my sister who died in childhood. I loved her long ago, and now I know I can love her forever. You, dear Libby, are the only woman I have ever loved—only you. I've loved you for a long time, but I didn't know how to express it. Without you in my life, nothing else makes sense. I love you, Liberty Taylor, and I've loved Anna since the first time I saw her in the hospital on Christmas Eve. When I learned she had no parents, I knew I had to do something about it. With the Christiansons' help, I'm trying to become her guardian and conservator while some arrangements can be made for adoption. But I'm afraid it's probably too late."

"Not yet," John interrupted. "If you will sign these papers, my boy, we'll find a fax machine, and my friends at the courthouse will take care of the rest."

Desmond signed the papers and then turned to Libby. "Well, will you have me to be your companion forever?"

Libby searched Desmond's brown eyes.

She glanced back at Gran, who nodded her approval. "Yes—oh yes. I want to be your wife more than anything."

Loud cheers and applause erupted. Even the people in the reception area cheered.

Desmond led the procession of people to the tiny rose-colored chapel. On the front bench inside rested one sleeping child, who awoke when the doors opened. She rubbed her tired eyes and grinned at Libby and Desmond.

"Anna—how did you . . ." Desmond rushed to hold her.

"Gran brought me here to show me where Libby works and to help cheer her up. But what are you doing here?"

Libby and Desmond explained everything to Anna. She finally believed that she would have a family of her own. She hugged them both and then turned quietly to the stained glass window. "Thanks," she whispered. "I'll always believe."

"Let's go home," Desmond smiled. "He came, you know."

Anna and Libby looked puzzled. "Who came?" Anna asked.

"Santa Claus, of course." Desmond chuckled.

After the crowd cleared, the new little family lingered, embracing in the fading light of dusk. They turned to leave, and Desmond studied the chapel, carving every precious detail in his memory. He noticed that a small pair of well-worn red woolen mittens had been curiously left behind on the pulpit. On the floor nearest the window, Desmond found a handwritten note that read:

On this night, we end one more year;
Carving new memories, putting away fear.
Reaching, touching, gathering miracles to share,
Remembering the Carpenter who taught us to care.

At last they had found one another. In the midst of a sometimes cold and uncaring world, three lonely souls experienced a single act of kindness that set in motion a chain of events culminating in a loving and eternal alteration of their lives. It was a miracle, and the small family knew that their feelings would live forever.

A Note to the Reader

C. S. Lewis writes of a place called Narnia, where it is always winter and never Christmas. In contrast, we long for a world where it is always Christmas and never winter in the hearts and minds of men. In our longing, the evergreen tree has become a symbol of hope, reminding us of life's everlasting treasures. Under our Christmas evergreens each year, we collect memories—priceless, eternal gifts. And each of these memories holds a miracle greater than any fleeting gratification worldly gifts can offer. The evergreen reminds us of life's everlasting treasures—love, relationships, belief.

Each season as we carefully put away our Christmas evergreens, we store our precious memories, and commit once again to collect and remember the love of Christmas throughout each year and always. For it is in well-made memories that we find the miracle of eternity, and therein lies the hope that enables us again and again to believe.